A MANIFESTO FOR MEDIA FREEDOM

A Manifesto for Media Freedom

Brian C. Anderson
and
Adam D. Thierer

Encounter Books
New York · London

First edition published in 2008 by Encounter Books, an activity of Encounter for Culture and Education, Inc., a nonprofit, tax exempt corporation. Encounter Books website address: www.encounterbooks.com

Manufactured in the United States and printed on acid-free paper. The paper used in this publication meets the minimum requirements of ANSI/NISO z39.48–1992 (R 1997) (*Permanence of Paper*).

FIRST EDITION

Parts of this book have been expanded and adapted from material that first appeared in *City Journal*.

LIBRARY OF CONGRESS CATALOGING-IN-PUBLICATION DATA

Anderson, Brian C., 1961–
A manifesto for media freedom / Brian C. Anderson and Adam D. Thierer.
p.   cm.
Includes bibliographical references and index.
ISBN-13: 978-1-59403-228-8 (hardcover : alk. paper)
ISBN-10: 1-59403-228-9 (hardcover : alk. paper)
1. Mass media—Political aspects—United States. 2. Freedom of speech—United States. I. Thierer, Adam D. II. Title.
P95.82.U6A53 2008
323.44′50973—dc22
2008032352

10 9 8 7 6 5 4 3 2 1

CONTENTS

For Myron Magnet – B C A

To my kids, the future of freedom – A D T

PREFACE

Why a manifesto for media freedom? The short answer: because it's necessary.

America today offers a breathtaking abundance of new and old media outlets for obtaining news, information, and entertainment: newspapers and magazines; radio and satellite radio; video broadcast through airwaves, sent through cables, or watched on DVDs or the Internet; blogs and websites of all kinds; and on and on. Yet many people—especially liberals, including party leaders from Barack Obama to Howard Dean to Hillary Clinton—hate this profusion, and never more than when it involves political speech. The current media market, they charge, doesn't represent true diversity, or isn't fair, or is subject to manipulation by a small and shrinking group of media barons. They want the government to regulate it into better shape, which just happens to be a shape that benefits them.

Doing so, we argue in the chapters ahead, would be a disaster, a kind of soft or not-so-soft tyranny that would wipe out whole sectors of media, curtailing free speech and impoverishing our democracy. Those on the right should be particularly outraged by this threat, for conservatives and libertarians have benefited hugely from the expanded mediasphere. Look at talk radio, which the right dominates, or the Web, where conservatives compete robustly with liberal and leftist alternatives. Nothing like these options existed a quarter-century ago, when most news and information outlets were at least implicitly sympathetic with a liberal worldview.

We also believe that a wake-up call on media freedom is crucial now because the Democratic left seems poised to increase its hold on Congress. Should a Democrat take the White House in November 2008 as well, an array of new media regulations would be almost certain. And whatever the election outcome, unless Americans understand what is happening, the pressure for new regulations isn't going to go away. Such an understanding isn't easy to come by, because the issues are complex and the agencies involved—especially the Federal Communications Commission and the Federal Election Commission—are mysterious in their operations and language. Thus we have tried to write about the threat to media freedom as clearly and accessibly as possible.

We open with a quick survey of the wildly diverse modern media universe and of the main philosophical and political objections to it. The left seems certain that a media problem ails our society; it just can't decide what that problem is. Some contend that real media choices are as limited or biased as ever, while others argue that our democracy is imperiled by *too many* media choices, making it hard to share common thoughts or feelings. What unites these two types of critics is their elitist presumption that they know what's best for the rest of us. They would love to rewrite regulations to tilt the media in the direction they prefer; and if they are allowed to do so, what is shaping up to be America's Golden Age of media could come to a sudden end.

In Chapter Two, we consider a regulatory favorite of the left: the outrageously misnamed "Fairness Doctrine." Ronald Reagan's rejection of the doctrine in the 1980s opened the way for an abundance of conservative and libertarian viewpoints on the air; and the left has been clamoring for its reinstatement ever since. Even though the FCC's decades-long enforcement of the Fairness Doctrine had clearly exercised a "chilling effect" on public speech and debate, the left continues to advocate its revival as a way to "balance" viewpoints on the airwaves, using the threat of FCC fines and regulation of licensed TV and radio broadcasters. Some liberals suggest that even a new Fairness Doctrine wouldn't be enough to correct a "structural imbalance" in the media marketplace. They want tightened ownership regulations, mandates ensuring "greater local accountability" over radio and TV broadcasters, and a significant ramping up of subsidies for public radio and TV stations. One leading leftist proposal would even force private broadcasters to fund public broadcasters! These proposals expose the left's true goal: to regulate private media outlets comprehensively and drive out those owners who dare to offer right-leaning alternatives.

Chapter Three surveys the left's aggressive push for so-called network neutrality, a requirement for "equal treatment" of the digital information surging through the Web—which would amount to a Fairness Doctrine for the Internet. Even though broadband competition is intensifying and there's no shortage of opinions and content available online, liberals have imagined a variety of dark scenarios in which the Internet as we know it will end unless government regulation comes to the rescue. But the real effect of such intervention—as was the case with the Fairness Doctrine—would likely be a stifling of online speech and a narrowing range of thought.

The fourth chapter explores another source of the regulatory impulse: what we call "neophobia," which sees only corruption and danger lurking in the new universe of video games, expanded television, and online social networking, and which supports Nanny State solutions for all these supposed evils. Many media critics both on the left and, regrettably, on the right believe that parents are essentially powerless in today's media world, so bureaucrats must step in to act on their behalf. Yet, as we will show, parents have more tools and methods at their disposal than ever before to make decisions about what is best for their own children. Empowered parents are better than empowered regulators.

In the final chapter, we take on the regulatory monster of campaign-finance reform—chiefly a product of the left but with some enthusiastic help from the current Republican presidential candidate, John McCain—which now creeps toward restricting political speech in the media. Campaign-finance reform has been promoted as a tool against corruption, even though such corruption does not seem to be widespread. In fact, it is vibrant political discourse that appears to be the real target of "reformers" and FEC regulators. Of all the threats to media freedom, modern campaign-finance regulations are perhaps the most dangerous because they strike directly at our First Amendment rights as citizens to engage in political debate.

In each of these cases, we advance a pro-freedom paradigm to counter the left's vision of media control. What do we mean

Preface

by the "media freedom" that we advocate as the alternative to these new regulatory crusades? For media consumers, it's the freedom to consume whatever information or entertainment we want from whatever sources we choose, without government restricting our choices. For media creators and distributors, it's the freedom to structure their business affairs as they wish in seeking to offer the public an expanding array of media options, for both news and entertainment. And for both consumers and creators, media freedom is being able to speak one's mind without restraint and without the threat of FCC or FEC bureaucrats telling us what is "fair."

We make no claim to be comprehensive in this brief book. We seek only to alert the American public to a growing peril to its freedom to watch, listen, and read what it wants—particularly when it comes to politics and, above all, when those politics happen to be on the right.

CHAPTER ONE

THE MEDIA CORNUCOPIA

AND ITS CRITICS

THROUGHOUT MOST OF HISTORY, humans lived in a state of extreme information poverty. News traveled slowly, field to field, village to village. Even after the advent of the printing press, information spread at a snail's pace. Few people knew how to find printed materials, assuming that they even knew how to read. Today, by contrast, we live in a world of unprecedented media abundance that once would have been the stuff of science-fiction novels. We can increasingly obtain and consume whatever media we want, wherever and whenever we want: television, radio, books (including electronic ones), newspapers, magazines, DVDs, video games, and the bewildering variety of material available on the Internet.

This media cornucopia is a wonderful development for a free society—or so you would think. But today's media universe has fierce detractors, and none more vehement than those on the left. Their criticisms seem contradictory, however. Some, such as Rep. Dennis Kucinich, claim that media choices are still too

I

LAYER 1 *Product or Content*	LAYER 2 *Distribution Mechanism*
Television programming	Broadcast TV stations
Movies	Cinemas, broadcast TV
Radio programming	Broadcast radio stations
Music	Radio, records, tapes
Print news & literature	Newspaper & magazine delivery
Advertising	TV, radio, mail, magazines
Telecommunications	Phone networks
Photography	Cameras

limited and sources of information too biased, and that these defects hinder citizens from participating fully in a deliberative democracy. Others argue that an excess of media choices today makes it too hard to build a democratic community. Both these liberal views are quite wrong.

Back in 2003, a somewhat free-market-minded Federal Communications Commission, chaired by Michael Powell, a Republican, proposed to revise the arcane policies governing media ownership, which, among other things, limit how many newspapers, television stations, or radio stations a single entity can own in each community. "Americans today have more media choices, more sources of news and information, and more varied entertainment programming available to them than ever before," the FCC observed.[1] Allowing slightly more cross-ownership, it reasoned, would simply clear out the regulatory deadwood that artificially restricted the ability of older media operators (broadcasters and newspapers) to compete

LAYER 3 *Receiving or Display Mechanism*	LAYER 4 *Personal Storage Tool*
TV sets	None
Movie theaters	None
Radios, stereos	None
Radio, reel-to-reel tape decks, stereos	Records & tapes
Newsprint, books	Books, personal libraries
All of the above	Rarely stored
Telephones	None
Print film	Film / prints

with all the new media alternatives. Such a measure would do nothing to hurt media multiplicity.

Despite the moderate nature of the FCC's proposal, all hell broke loose on the left, and things haven't really calmed down since. In congressional debates, Democratic lawmakers warned apocalyptically of the horrors that the FCC's proposed reform would unleash. Rep. Edward Markey of Massachusetts—mentioning *Citizen Kane* but clearly thinking of Rupert Murdoch, whose FOX News and other media outlets have won a big audience for conservative views—implied that a few all-powerful media tycoons could soon run the world.[2] Rep. Lynn Woolsey of California accused the FCC of trying to impose a centralized "Saddam-style information system in the United States."[3] Not to be outdone, New York's Maurice Hinchey saw the new rules as a GOP-led "mind control" project. "It's a well-thought-out and planned effort to control the political process," he said. "It will wipe out our democracy."[4] Howard Dean, a Democratic

LAYER 1 *Product or Content*	LAYER 2 *Distribution Mechanism*
Video / television	Broadcast, cable & satellite TV; Internet sites & online stores, VHS tapes, DVDs, PPV, VOD, mobile, P2P
Movies	Cinemas, broadcast cable & satellite TV, Internet sites & online stores, camcorders, VHS tapes, DVDs, PPV, VOD, mobile, P2P
Audio / music	Broadcast radio, satellite radio (XM & Sirius), Internet sites & online stores, podcasts, P2P
Print news & literature	Newspaper & magazine delivery, Internet sites, software, mobile devices
Advertising	TV, radio, mail, magazines, broadcast, cable & satellite TV, mobile devices & PDAs
Telecommunications	Phone networks, mobile networks, cable networks, Internet telephony (VoIP), IM
Online content & services	Phone, cable, and wireless networks; IM, portals, blogs, search engines, social networking sites, RSS aggregators
Video games	Video game platforms, discs, computer software, Internet & online stores, mobile networks
Photography	Digital cameras, camcorders, mobile devices & PDAs, Internet & online stores

presidential candidate at the time, vowed to break up Murdoch's media empire "on ideological grounds."[5]

The circus-like "town hall meetings" that followed were even more overheated. Pushed by Democratic FCC commissioners and organized by MoveOn.org, Free Press, and other leftist

LAYER 3 *Receiving or Display Mechanism*	LAYER 4 *Personal Storage Tool*
TV sets & computer monitors, mobile & handheld devices	PVRs (i.e., TiVo), VCRs, DVDs, computer discs & hard drives, online storage
Cinemas, TV sets, computer monitors, personal digital devices	VCRs, DVDs, computer discs & hard drives, online storage
Home & car radios, stereos, iPods, MP3 players & other personal digital devices, PDAs	CDs, tapes, personal digital devices, computer discs & hard drives, online storage
Newsprint, books, PCs, Internet sites, mobile devices & PDAs	Books, personal libraries, PDAs, computer discs & hard drives, online storage, printers
Almost anything	Rarely stored
Telephones, cell phones, PDAs, TV sets	Voice mail, online services
Computer monitors, PDAs, cell phones, TV sets	Computer discs & hard drives, online storage, personal digital devices
TV sets & computer monitors, handheld gaming units, mobile devices & PDAs	CDs/DVDs, computer discs & hard drives
Print film, computers, TV sets, mobile devices & PDAs	Prints, CDs/DVDs, memory cards, computer discs & hard drives, online storage, printers

advocacy groups, these sessions gave anyone with a gripe against a media company a chance to vent. Some grumbled that TV and radio featured too much religious programming; others argued that there wasn't enough. Everyone said that local radio broadcast nothing but garbage, but everyone defined garbage differently. And many aired long lists of complaints about the multiple radio stations, television channels, and newspapers in their areas, only to conclude that their local media markets were insufficiently competitive!

The critics did agree on one thing: government had to take steps to remedy our current media predicament—whatever it was. A variety of advocacy groups then took the FCC to court and got the Third Circuit Court of Appeals to put the whole media-ownership revision on hold.

Most participants in the town hall meetings fell into the scarcity-obsessed camp. On the face of it, the scarcity critics have a tough case to make. According to FCC data and various private reports, America boasts nearly 14,000 radio stations today, double the number that were operating in 1970. Satellite radio—an industry that didn't even exist before 2001—claimed roughly 16 million subscribers nationwide by 2007.[6] Today, 86 percent of households subscribe to cable or satellite TV, receiving an average of 102 channels of the more than 500 available to them.[7] There were 19,419 magazines produced in 2006, up from 14,302 in 1993.[8] The only declining media sector is the newspaper business, which has seen circulation erode for many years now. But that is largely a result of the competition that it faces from other outlets.[9]

Throw the Internet into the mix and you get dizzy. The Internet Systems Consortium reports that the number of Internet host computers—the computers or servers that allow people to post content on the Web—has grown from just 235 in 1982 to 1.3 million in 1993 to roughly 500 million in 2007.[10] As of April 2008, the blog-tracking service Technorati counted over 112 million blogs, with more than 175,000 new ones created

Number of Broadcast Radio Stations 1921–2007

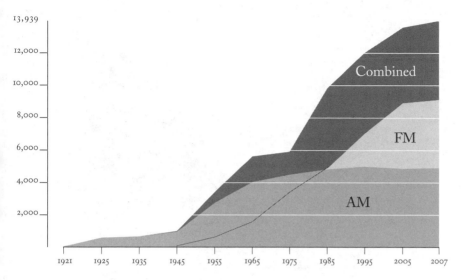

Source: Federal Communications Commission

Total Number of Broadcast TV Stations 1941–2007

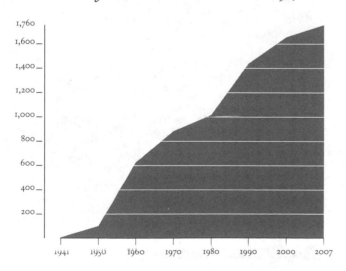

Source: Federal Communications Commission

7

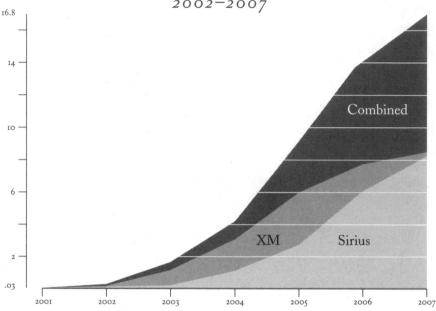

16.8

14

Combined

10

6

XM   Sirius

2

.03

2001   2002   2003   2004   2005   2006   2007

Source: Various Sirius and XM annual reports

Video Choices & Vertical Integration
in the Multichannel Video Marketplace

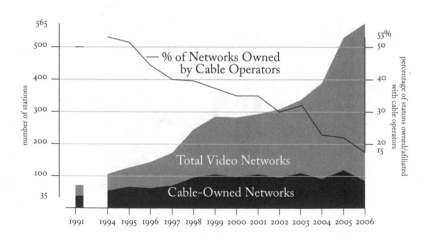

565

500

53%
50

% of Networks Owned
by Cable Operators

400   40

number of stations

300   30

percentage of stations owned/affiliated
with cable operators

200   20
                                                                   15

Total Video Networks

100

Cable-Owned Networks

35

1991 1994 1995 1996 1997 1998 1999 2000 2001 2002 2003 2004 2005 2006

Sources: Federal Communications Commission, various Annual Video Competition reports
Data not available for 1991–1993

Household Penetration Rates for Various Technologies

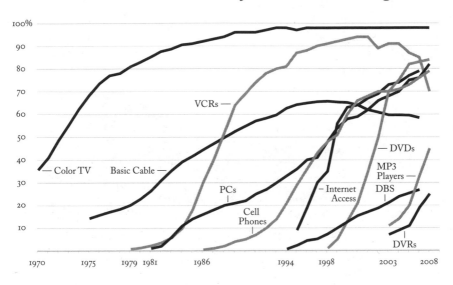

Sources: US Department of Commerce, Census Bureau, Consumer Electronics Association,
National Cable and Telecommunications Association, Nielsen/Net Ratings

Number of Years It Took for Major Technologies to Reach 50% of Homes

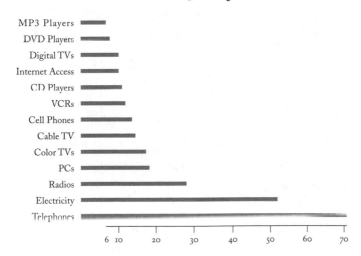

Sources: Census Bureau, Consumer Electronics Association, National Cable and
Telecommunications Association

Growth of Blogs 2003–2008

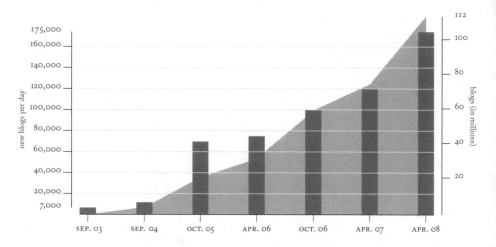

Source: Technorati; Dave Sifry

daily. Bloggers update their sites "to the tune of over 1.6 million posts per day, or over 18 updates a second," according to Technorati.[11]

But the scarcity critics have a rejoinder: the apparent diversity isn't real, because a handful of media barons—hell-bent on force-feeding us their politically reactionary pabulum and commercial messages—control most of it (even before any changes in ownership rules by the FCC). "You can literally say you actually have more voices, but they are the same voices increasingly," says Ken Auletta, media writer for *The New Yorker*.[12] Even the Internet isn't what it's cracked up to be, the argument goes. In *Media Ownership and Democracy in the Digital Information Age*, Mark Cooper, director of research at the Consumer Federation of America, lambastes the Internet for failing to serve "the public interest," for being too commercial, for not helping local communities, for hurting deliberative democracy, and for failing to enhance citizens' ability "to define themselves

Average Prices for Selected Technologies 2003–2008

	2003	2004	2005	2006	2007	2008 (est.)	Price Reduction
Digital television sets	$1,571	1537	1369	995	954	917	-41.60%
Direct broadcast satellite	$120	105	98	92	87	782	-31.70%
VCRs	$63	57	58	59	48	43	-31.70%
DVD players	$123	109	110	100	72	69	-43.90%
DVD recorders		271	212	198	178	159	-41.30%
Next-gen DVD players				500	395	307	-38.60%
Digital video recorders	$261	190	168	196	177	160	-38.70%
IPTV		175	150	136	127	119	-32.00%
MP3 players	$140	181	170	146	118	116	-17.10%

and their place in everyday life."[13] Who knew that the Internet was so harmful to modern society?

It's all nonsense, starting with the notion that a tiny group has a stranglehold on the media. A 2002 FCC survey of ten media markets—from the largest (New York City) to the smallest (Altoona, Pennsylvania)—showed that each had more outlets and owners in 2000 than in 1960. And because the FCC counted all of a market's cable channels as a single outlet (while the typical viewer would regard each channel as a distinct entity) and didn't include national newspapers or Internet sites as media sources, the diversity picture was even brighter than the survey results suggested. Ben Compaine, a media theorist who

Comparison of Media Outlets and Owners
for Ten Selected Media Markets, 1960–2000

Market Rank	City	1960 Outlets	Owners
1	New York, NY	89	60
29	Kansas City, MO	22	16
57	Birmingham, AL	28	20
85	Little Rock, AR	17	14
113	Lancaster, PA	14	10
141	Burlington, VT / Plattsburgh, NY	15	13
169	Myrtle Beach, SC	6	6
197	Terre Haute, IN	12	8
225	Charlottesville, VA	8	5
253	Altoona, PA	11	9

Source: Federal Communications Commission, Media Ownership Working Group, September 2002

has studied the issue closely, observed: "I have never heard a convincing argument that any individual in the United States ... cannot easily and inexpensively have access to a huge variety of news, information, opinion, culture, and entertainment, whether from 10, 50, or 3,000 sources. If that is what passes for media concentration, we should consider ourselves pretty lucky."[14]

Nor do Americans lack a rich variety of "voices" in the media. Each new commercial media outlet must provide something at least slightly different from its rivals. If every book,

1980		2000		Change	
Outlets	Owners	Outlets	Owners	Outlets	Owners
154	116	184	114	107%	90%
44	33	53	33	141%	106%
44	34	59	38	111%	90%
35	30	60	33	253%	136%
21	16	25	20	79%	100%
37	28	53	34	253%	162%
22	16	38	23	533%	283%
26	19	33	22	175%	175%
13	10	23	14	188%	180%
19	12	23	15	109%	67%
				195%	139%

magazine, TV channel, radio program, and website really said the same thing, citizens wouldn't bother consuming more than one or two of them, and we wouldn't have the media abundance that we enjoy today.

Becoming an informed citizen has never been easier. You can get up in the morning and still read your (probably liberal) local paper and several national ones—say, the *Wall Street Journal* (right-of-center editorial page) and *USA Today* (more or less centrist). Walk to the newsstand and you've got political mag-

Cable and Satellite TV Programming Options

NEWS

CNN, Fox News, MSNBC, C-SPAN, C-SPAN 2, C-SPAN 3, BBC America, ABC News Now, CNN International

SPORTS

Sports: ESPN, ESPN 2, ESPN News, ESPN Classics, Fox Sports, TNT, NBA TV, NFL Network, Golf Channel, Tennis Channel, Speed Channel, Outdoor Life Network, Fuel

HOME RENOVATION

Home & Garden Television, The Learning Channel, DIY, Style

WEATHER

The Weather Channel, Weatherscan

EDUCATIONAL / INFORMATIONAL / TRAVEL

History Channel, Biography Channel (A&E), The Learning Channel (TLC), Discovery Channel, National Geographic Channel, Animal Planet, Science Channel, The Travel Channel

FINANCIAL

CNNfn, CNBC, Fox Business Network, Bloomberg Television

FEMALE-ORIENTED

WE (Women's Entertainment), Oxygen, Lifetime Television, Lifetime Real Women, Lifetime Movie Network, Showtime Women, SoapNet

FAMILY / CHILDREN-ORIENTED

Animal Planet, Anime Network, ABC Family, Black Family Channel, Boomerang, Cartoon Network, Discovery Kids, Disney Channel, Familyland Television Network, FUNimation, Hallmark Channel, Hallmark Movie Channel, HBO Family, KTV-Kids and Teens Television, Nickelodeon, Nick 2, Nick Toons, Noggin (2–5 years), The N Channel (9–14 years), PBS Kids Sprout, Showtime Family Zone, Starz! Kids & Family, Toon Disney, Varsity TV, WAM (movies for 8–16-year-olds), GAS, American Life TV, Family Net

SHOPPING

The Shopping Channel, Home Shopping Network, QVC, Jewelry, Shop NBC

AFRICAN AMERICAN

BET, Black Starz! Black Family Channel, BET Gospel,

FOREIGN / FOREIGN LANGUAGE

Telemundo (Spanish), Univision (Spanish), Deutsche Welle (German), BBC America (British), AIT: African Independent Television, TV Asia, ZEE-TV Asia (South Asia), ART: Arab Radio and Television, CCTV-4: China Central Television, The Filipino Channel (Philippines), Saigon Broadcasting Network (Vietnam), Channel One Russian Worldwide Network, The International Channel, HBO Latino, History Channel en Español

RELIGIOUS

Trinity Broadcasting Network, The Church Channel (TBN), World Harvest Television, Eternal Word Television Network (EWTN), National Jewish Television, Worship Network

MUSIC

MTV, MTV 2, MTV Jams, MTV Hits, VH1, VH1 Classic, VH1 Megahits, VH1 Soul, VH1 Country, Fuse, Country Music Television (CMT), CMT Pure Country Great American Country, Great American Country, Gospel Music Television Network

MOVIES

HBO, Showtime, Cinemax, Starz, Encore, The Movie Channel, Turner Classic Movies, AMC, IFC, Flix, Sundance, Bravo (action, westerns, mystery, love stories, etc.)

OTHER OR GENERAL-INTEREST PROGRAMMING

TBS, USA Network, TNT, F/X, SciFi Channel, Spike TV, truTV, Sleuth, Crime & Investigation Network, Wealth TV, TV One

Source: Federal Communications Commission, various Annual Video Competition reports

Radio Stations per Format

Format	Count	Format	Count
Country	1704	Active Rock	142
News / Talk / Information	1503	Spanish Contemporary	134
Religious	948	Educational	133
Adult Contemporary	822	Ethnic	99
Oldies	780	New Country	96
Variety	748	Contemporary Inspirational	90
Contemporary Christian	677	Jazz	74
All Sports	527	New AC / Smooth Jazz	72
Classic Rock	512	Nostalgia	70
Hot Adult Contemporary	447	Spanish Religious	68
Pop Contemporary Hits	386	Spanish News / Talk	61
Alternative	321	Children's Radio	56
Gospel	320	Easy Listening	49
Adult Standards	314	Spanish Adult Hits	49
Classical	291	Spanish Tropical	49
Classic Country	287	All News	36
Mexican Regional	277	Modern Adult Contemporary	35
Classic Hits	264	'80s Hits	27
Talk / Personality	204	Spanish Oldies	27
Album-Oriented Rock (AOR)	197	Tejano	25
Southern Gospel	190	Rhythmic Oldies	21
Urban Contemporary	171	Urban Oldies	19
Urban Adult Contemporary	171	Latino Urban	6
Rhythmic Contemporary Hits	167	Grupera	4
Soft Adult Contemporary	155	Hablados / Noticiarios	2
Spanish Variety	145	Variada Musical / Noticiarios	2
Adult Hits	144	Español Catalogo	1
Album Adult Alternative	144	Other	77

Source: Arbitron

azines galore, from the Marxist *New Left Review* to the paleocon *American Conservative*. On cable and satellite television: CNN, MSNBC, CNBC, FOX News, PBS, local news, the big networks (at least for now), the BBC, C-SPAN, community access shows—all offer a wide variety of news and information options, some around the clock. Turn on the car radio, and Rush Lim-

New Magazine Launches by Genre, 2002–2006

Metro / Region / State	229	Fishing / Hunting	23
Special Interest	115	Literary Reviews / Writing	22
Ethnic / Black	95	Teen	16
Home Service / Home	85	Photography	15
Women's	57	Media Personalities	13
Fashion / Beauty /		Military/ Naval	11
Grooming	52	Camping /	
Health	49	Outdoor Recreation	10
Business / Finance	40	Boating / Yachting	8
Pop Culture	37	Science / Technology	6
Babies	35	Gardening	5
Men's	31	Nature / Ecology	2
Children's	30		
Religious / Denominational	27	*Source: Magazine Publishers of America*	

baugh or Sean Hannity booms out at you from the right, or maybe you can tune in to Sirius Left on satellite.

The Internet has done more than any other technology to create the sort of media that scarcity critics claim to desire. Today, every man, woman, and child can have a "newspaper" or broadcast outlet—that is, a website, blog, or podcast. It's hard to imagine how the political blogosphere could be more diverse, ranging from the Daily Kos and the Huffington Post on the left to National Review Online and Power Line and FrontPage on the right, with Andrew Sullivan, Instapundit, and Buzz Machine somewhere in between. A political junkie must hustle to keep up with what RealClearPolitics posts on its site every day.

The same breathtaking abundance characterizes entertainment and lifestyle media, which now provide something for every interest under the sun. Consider a truly eclectic person: a lesbian feminist African American who likes to hunt on weekends and has a passion for country music. Would the "mainstream media" of twenty-five years ago have represented any of her interests? Unlikely. Today, though, this woman can program her TiVo to record her favorite shows on Black Entertainment Television, Logo (a gay/lesbian-oriented cable channel), Oxygen (female-targeted programming), the Outdoor Life Network, and Country Music Television. "We've gone from a few programmers in New York and Los Angeles deciding what people will watch to the people themselves voting with their remote controls every night, really every minute, on what they want," says David Westin, president of ABC News.[15] And that's just television.

The scarcity worrywarts thus ignore a recent history of stunning technological innovation and marketplace evolution that has made us as information-rich as any society in history. But this is where a second group of leftist media critics enters the picture.

"What information consumes is rather obvious: the attention of its recipients," remarked the Nobel Prize–winning economist and psychologist Herbert Simon in 1971. "Hence a wealth of information creates a poverty of attention, and a need to allocate that attention efficiently among the overabundance of information sources that might consume it."[16] Decades later, confronting a "wealth of information" that Simon could not have imagined, a growing group of left-wing critics warn about its destructive consequences. The titles of recent books by Todd Gitlin and Barry Schwartz—*Media Unlimited: How the Torrent of Images and Sounds Overwhelms Our Lives* and *The Paradox of Choice: Why More Is Less*, respectively—capture the anxiety felt by these opponents of media multiplicity.[17] There is just too much information!

Yet even if one concedes that the number of media choices can be daunting, notes Chris Anderson, editor of *Wired* magazine, the market is responding. In his 2006 bestseller, *The Long Tail*, Anderson celebrates the explosion of information-sorting intermediaries and filtering tools that enable us to take full advantage of the media cornucopia.[18] Google, Netflix, Amazon.com, and iTunes are just a few examples, or RealClearPolitics and Huffington Post for political information. "These technologies and services sift through a vast array of choices to present you with the ones that are most right for you," Anderson points out.

But according to one of the most influential abundance-is-bad media critics, Cass Sunstein, those filters only make things worse. In his 2001 book *Republic.com*, Sunstein, a liberal law professor, remarks that the hyper-customization of specialized websites and online technologies enables Americans to create a highly personalized information retrieval service—a "Daily Me," he calls it, using a term coined by Nicholas Negroponte, a technology theorist.[19] But whereas Negroponte, like Anderson, welcomes filtering and specialization as a liberating break from traditional, force-fed media, Sunstein believes that they cause social fragmentation and alienation, which in turn could feed political extremism. "A system of limitless individual choices, with respect to communications, is not necessarily in the interest of citizenship and self-government," he writes.[20]

Schwartz echoes the point, fearing the antisocial effects of a media world that offers "choice without boundaries." "In a decade or so, when [TiVos] are in everybody's home," he writes ruefully, "it's a good bet that when folks gather around the watercooler to discuss the last night's big TV events, no two of them will have watched the same shows."[21] Similarly, Bill Carrick, a media advisor to the former Democratic presidential candidate Richard Gephardt, complained a while back to the *Washington Post* that the rise of the Internet, cable, and other new media was making it hard for politicians to reach the masses with their campaign messages. "The danger for democracy," he asserted, "is that we're losing the universal campfire."[22] Marc Gunther of *Fortune* magazine bemoans "the extinction of mass culture" as a result of the new media, which he claims have polarized the country politically.[23]

When Sunstein and other liberal information-overload critics bemoan the loss of a "universal campfire" or shared watercooler experiences, they are implicitly making the point that we were better off with only a few media outlets. Some openly wax nostalgic about a Golden Age of newspapers, radio, and television, when supposedly we were less distracted, better informed, and enjoyed a better sense of community. This Norman Rockwell view is far more myth than reality. Was American democracy really better off when William Randolph Hearst dominated the newspaper business, or when the Big Three television networks brought us the news at a set time each night? And was community really stronger when everyone talked about the same things around the nation's watercoolers every day? Go back to the founding era and you'll find a polemical and partisan throng of fiery, often calumnious pamphleteers (not unlike today's bloggers), as well as publishers beholden to patrons.[24]

One can make a strong case that the new media—and the Internet, above all—are facilitating a more rigorous deliberative democracy and a richer sense of community. "In modern American political history, perhaps only the coming of the television age has had as big an impact on our national elections as the Internet has," observes Raul Fernandez, chief executive of the software firm ObjectVideo. "But the effect of the Internet may be better for the long-term health of our democracy. For while TV emphasizes perception, control, and centralization, Internet-driven politics is about transparency, distribution of effort, and, most important, empowerment and participation—at whatever level of engagement the consumer wants."[25]

As for community, "the Digital Age hasn't mechanized humanity and isolated people in a sterile world of machines," believes Richard Saul Wurman, author of *Information Anxiety*.[26] Instead, it has enabled people around the globe to band together, especially via the Internet, and communicate in ways previously unimaginable.

What the two differing schools of leftist media criticism have in common is pure elitism. Media abundance (which the scarcity critics must implausibly wave away as a mirage) has meant lots more room for right-of-center viewpoints that, while popular with many Americans, are unacceptable to the critics. The fact that Bill O'Reilly gets better ratings than Bill Moyers perturbs them to no end.

Both liberal groups would love to put their thumbs on the scale and tilt the media in their preferred direction. Scarcity-obsessed Dennis Kucinich has recently introduced plans in Congress to revive the Fairness Doctrine, which, as we will see in detail in the next chapter, once let government regulators police the airwaves to ensure a balance of viewpoints—however that may be defined. A new Fairness Doctrine would most directly affect opinion-based talk radio, a medium that just happens to be dominated by conservatives. Sunstein, who advises leading Democrats on regulatory and legal issues, also proposes a kind of speech redistributionism. For the Internet, he suggests that regulators could impose "electronic sidewalks" on partisan websites (such as the National Rifle Association site), forcing them to link to opposing views. The practical problems of implementing this program would be forbidding, even if it somehow proved constitutional. How many links to opposing views would secure the government's approval? The FCC would need an army of media regulators (much as China has today)[27] to monitor the millions of webpages, blogs, and social networking sites, and to keep them in line.

That leftist media critics start sounding so authoritarian is no surprise. In a media cornucopia, freedom of choice inevitably yields media inequality. "In systems where many people are free to choose between many options, a small subset of the whole will get a disproportionate amount of traffic (or attention, or income), even if no members of the system actively work towards such an outcome," writes Clay Shirky of New York University's Interactive Telecommunications Program.[28] Overcoming that inequality would require a completely regulated media.

When Rush Limbaugh has more listeners than NPR, and Tom Clancy sells more books than Noam Chomsky, and *Motor Trend* gets more subscribers than *Mother Jones*, liberals want to convince us (or themselves, perhaps) that it's all because of some catastrophic market failure or a grand corporate conspiracy to dumb down the masses. In reality, it's just the result of consumer choice. All the opinions that the left's media critics favor are now readily available to us on multiple platforms. But that's not good enough, it seems: they won't rest until all of us are watching, reading, and listening to the content that they prefer.

In the next two chapters, we will zero in on the real-world consequences of the mistaken ideas about media, government, and society that we have canvassed here, first looking at the left's campaign to bring back the Fairness Doctrine, then moving on to the controversy over "network neutrality"—a policy intended to establish "equal treatment" for all the information bits that move across the Web.

CHAPTER TWO

THE UNFAIRNESS DOCTRINE

THE LEFT, watching uneasily as power drains away daily from the CBS Newses and *Time* magazines of the mediasphere, clearly understands the revolutionary implications of the media cornucopia. Instead of fighting back with ideas, however, many of today's liberals are quietly, relentlessly, and illiberally working to smother this flourishing universe of political discourse under a tangle of new government regulations. While those on the political right have the most to lose in the short run, all Americans who care about our fundamental rights and the civic health of our democracy need to understand what's going on.

In its highest-profile effort to shut down the political speech it doesn't like, the left is working to restore the Fairness Doctrine or some kind of regulatory analogue. Make no mistake: this would wipe out most political talk radio and possibly conservative-friendly FOX News, too.

For those who don't remember, the Federal Communications Commission's Fairness Doctrine, formalized as an agency regulation in the late 1940s but dating back in various forms to 1929, required radio and then broadcast television stations to cover "vitally important controversial issues of interest in the community served by the broadcaster" and at the same time to provide "opportunity for the presentation of contrasting viewpoints on such issues."

The language sounds anodyne, but in practice it had a huge influence on how broadcasters operated. Those who didn't follow these rules could face FCC fines, be forced to give free time to voices that federal regulators felt hadn't gotten fair treatment, and even lose their operating licenses. With tapes and other evidence in hand, FCC staff investigating complaints would "pull out stopwatches," said Jim McKinney, who once headed the commission's Mass Media Bureau. "They would start timing how many minutes and seconds a broadcaster devoted to the issue of public importance. And then, depending on how that came out, they would either close the investigation, or they would prepare an item for the commission to take an enforcement action."[1]

Concern that particular partisan views could dominate what was then a limited broadcast spectrum, which government felt it had to parcel out with the public interest in mind, drove this meddling—amounting to a partial nationalization of the airwaves. According to Dennis Patrick, former FCC chairman, and Thomas Hazlett, an economist and media scholar, the doctrine rested on "the presumption that government regulators can coolly review editorial choices and, with the power to license (or not license) stations, improve the quantity and quality of broadcast news." This presumption was erroneous, as it turns out, since every regulatory move by the commission triggered a political eruption.[2]

Civil libertarian Nat Hentoff remembers what it was like to

be a broadcaster in the old days. "I was in radio under the reign of the Fairness Doctrine, at WMEX in Boston in the 1940s and early '50s," he recalled in a talk at Hillsdale College. "We did not have any of the present-day contentious talk radio shows, but we covered politics and politicians," he continued, noting that he would occasionally offer political opinions on air, even on his jazz and folk music programs. "Suddenly Fairness Doctrine letters started coming in from the FCC and our station's front office panicked. Lawyers had to be summoned; tapes of accused broadcasters had to be examined with extreme care; voluminous responses had to be prepared and sent. After a few of these FCC letters, our boss announced that there would be no more controversy of any sort on WMEX. We had been muzzled."[3]

Even before the codification of the Fairness Doctrine in 1949, the government's power to award licenses to broadcasters proved too tempting *not* to abuse. Back in the twenties, for instance, Herbert Hoover as secretary of commerce distributed spectrum rights disproportionately to pro-business license seekers, whom he found to represent the "public interest" far more than labor groups.[4] The FCC almost snuffed out the Yankee Radio network in the late thirties after it began running hard-hitting conservative editorials, and let the stations stay on the air only after their owners agreed to stop the sermonizing.

The wielding of regulatory might for partisan ends really took off in the sixties, however, as former CBS president Fred Friendly documented in *The Good Guys, the Bad Guys, and the First Amendment*, an informative 1976 book on the Fairness Doctrine. An official in the Kennedy administration and the Democratic Party, Bill Ruder, acknowledged: "Our massive strategy was to use the Fairness Doctrine to challenge and harass the right-wing broadcasters, and hope that the challenges would be so costly to them that they would be inhibited and decide it was too costly to continue." Martin Firestone, a party activist, elaborated on the strategy in a confidential 1964 report to the Democratic National Committee, happily describing the 1,035 letters that were sent to conservative stations as part of this effort, which generated 1,678 hours of free time. These stations, mostly rural, were small and cash-starved, so they proved easy to browbeat. "Were our efforts to be continued on a year-round basis, we would find that many of these stations would consider the broadcasts of these programs bothersome and burdensome ... and would start dropping the programs from their broadcast schedule," Firestone wrote. DNC staffer Wayne Phillips added: "Even more important than the free radio time was the effectiveness of this operation in inhibiting the political activity of these right-wing broadcasts."[5]

The Nixon administration went after its critics even more thuggishly. Nixon staffers, recounts the radio historian Jessie Walker, threatened to strip the licenses from TV and radio networks whose coverage of their boss they deemed "unfair" —a tactic that understandably spooked station execs.[6] Indeed, such harassment "became a regular item on the agenda at White House policy meetings," Thomas Hazlett observes. During the Vietnam War protests in the autumn of 1969, Nixon ordered his staff to take "specific action" against network news coverage twenty-one separate times. Facing critical Watergate coverage in the *Washington Post* three years later, Nixon told aides John Dean and H. R. Haldeman that the paper would have "damnable, damnable problems" if it didn't back off: "They have a television station . . . and they are going to have to get it renewed," he said darkly.[7] (Ironically, Ruder wound up on Nixon's infamous list of enemies. "Harassment is a two-edged sword," says Walker.)

Special-interest groups used the Fairness Doctrine to fight for various causes. In 1984, to take one of many examples, the FCC, lobbied by antinuclear activists, ruled that a New York television station had unfairly privileged nuclear power by running a paid ad in favor of constructing a new plant while saying no to a piece opposing it. And Fairness Doctrine challenges didn't have to win in order to have an effect. In 1981, Walker points out, Mayor Henry Maier of Milwaukee called in the FCC after a local T V station blasted his administration in more than a dozen editorials. The station won both in the FCC and later in the courts, but it had to shell out considerable legal fees.

All this monitoring and bullying seems unconstitutional. After all, the First Amendment says that Congress must make no law that abridges freedom of speech or the press. But the nation's highest court long believed otherwise when it came to the airwaves. The Supreme Court first established the legal grounds for using a "public interest" or "fairness" criterion to license and regulate broadcasters in *National Broadcasting Co. v. United States* in 1943. Writing for the majority, Justice Felix Frankfurter posited that scarce frequencies plus a private marketplace equaled a "cacophony of competing voices," with each electronic agent fighting to drown out the other; thus the government had a duty to ensure that all proceeded in an orderly fashion.[8]

The obvious rejoinder to Frankfurter is a single word: capitalism. Establishing property rights in frequencies would have regulated scarcity far more efficiently than government regulation could, and without the attendant risks of political abuse. Commercial radio had arrived in late 1920 and had grown rapidly in a free market, with hundreds of stations transmitting by the middle of the decade. The Commerce Department recognized broadcasters' exclusive rights with few complications, using a straightforward first-come, first-served system. Unfortunately, in 1926, the U.S. attorney general "upset the applecart," as Hazlett puts it, by nixing the department's power to grant rights in "the ether."[9] From 1927 on, the political sphere had dominion over broadcasting.

In an influential circuit court decision, Judge Robert Bork would later shred Frankfurter's contention that scarcity justified government regulation. "It is certainly true that broadcast frequencies are scarce," Bork wrote, "but it is unclear why that fact justifies content regulation of broadcasting in a way that would be intolerable if applied to the editorial process of the print media." All economic goods are scarce, Bork reasoned— "not least the newsprint, ink, delivery trucks, computers, and other resources that go into the production and dissemination of print journalism. Not everyone who wishes to publish a newspaper, or even a pamphlet, may do so."[10] Why would scarcity be irrelevant in one case and essential in the other? The number of broadcast TV stations has doubled since 1970 and now exceeds the number of daily papers, yet we don't have a Fairness Doctrine governing the *New York Times*.

Government ownership and control of spectrum aggravated—and indeed, helped cause—the very problem that it was intended to solve. While it's true that the overall amount of spectrum out there has some limit (which, as Bork noted, is the case with all resources), FCC regulation creates an artificial scarcity in several ways. When the agency initially allocates spectrum, for instance, it sets an overall cap on the amount available for the entire band of service (say, FM radio). But this cap is arbitrary. Why has the FM band remained stuck between 88 and 109 MHz for the past half-century? Because that's what the command-and-control FCC tells us it *must* be. The same kind of arbitrariness is true of the FCC's initial spectrum allocations for individual licenses. The agency's "zoning" rules on the scope and nature of each license may in fact be the biggest scarcity producer, since the rules keep entrepreneurs from using the spectrum flexibly or rededicating it to different, perhaps more effective, uses. In essence, an FCC broadcast license says that you may do X, *and only* X, with that spectrum allocation—even when the market might cry out for something different. Currently, for example, TV broadcast stations waste enormous amounts of energy pumping out broadcast signals, even though 86 percent of Americans now get television from cable, satellite, or telco providers (which, further, carry almost all those old broadcast stations). Why not let some creative broadcasters sell off excess spectrum or put it to some other use? Because the FCC says they can't; end of story. In sum, as Ithiel de Sola Pool argued in *Technologies of Freedom* in 1983, "The scheme of granting free licenses for use of a frequency band, though defended on the supposition that scarce channels had to be husbanded for the best social use, was in fact what created a scarcity." Pool concluded: "[I]t was policy, not physics, that led to the scarcity of frequencies. Those who believed otherwise fell into a simple error in economics."[11]

The Unfairness Doctrine

Regrettably, the Supreme Court succumbed to that faulty reasoning. In 1969, the Court determined in *Red Lion v. FCC* that scarcity reigned and that the Fairness Doctrine itself was constitutional. The case involved a Pennsylvania station, WGCB (Word of God, Christ, and the Bible), which in 1964 broadcast a polemic by a fire-breathing populist preacher named Billy James Hargis excoriating *Goldwater: Extremist on the Right*, a book authored by a sometime *Nation* writer, Fred Cook. DNC monitors enrolled in Bill Ruder's harassment campaign drafted Cook to file an FCC complaint demanding on-air response time. The commission ordered WGCB to let Cook respond, the station refused (though it offered to sell him airtime at the same rate that Hargis paid), and the whole mess eventually wound its way to the Supreme Court.

The Court ruled unanimously for the FCC and affirmed Frankfurter's dubious scarcity rationale. But it also qualified its backing of the Fairness Doctrine. One of the regulation's purposes, the justices explained, was to bring the public more controversial views on important issues. If the doctrine instead had "the net effect of reducing rather than enhancing the volume and quality of coverage," if it had a "chilling effect" on speech, the Court might rethink its constitutionality.[12]

As the Supreme Court should have seen at the time, the Fairness Doctrine *was*, in Hentoff's language, "muzzling" the political speech that democracy thrives on. The regulation made it hard to program political talk radio or television in the vein of Sean Hannity, Mark Levin, or Bill O'Reilly—rowdily opinionated, unafraid to name names, often informative, and, if you disagree with the host's politics, galling. If a station ran a show like Rush Limbaugh's, drawing upward of 20 million listeners a week, it would also have had to run a left-wing alternative, even if sponsors were scarce (as has been the case with ratings wreck Air America and other efforts at liberal radio today). Most media executives concluded that such programming would be too risky and kept opinion programs off the air altogether in favor of blander fare and what the journalist Bill Monroe has described as "timid, don't rock the boat coverage."[13] In 1980, radio talk shows of any kind numbered fewer than a hundred nationwide.

All that changed in the mid-eighties, when Ronald Reagan's free-market-minded FCC stopped enforcing the Fairness Doctrine and then jettisoned it entirely in 1987. Because the number of cable and satellite television and FM radio stations had shot up, the "new technological abundance," in media theorist Peter Huber's phrase, had robbed the doctrine of even the implausible "scarcity" rationale.[14] And it was clear to the commissioners that the doctrine was chilling free speech, too. "When you drop the requirement for free response time, when you remove the obligation to present significant contrasting views, when you remove the regulatory and financial risk associated with controversial editorials, when you stop taxing speech, you get more of it," said Dennis Patrick, the FCC chairman at the time, in a 2007 National Press Club talk.[15]

In fact, Patrick regarded the Fairness Doctrine as "unconstitutional on its face," though *Red Lion* has never been overturned. Broadcasters, he argued in his NPC address, are part of the press: "To suggest otherwise is to suggest the framers of our constitution intended to protect from federal coercion only those who used the technology of the day—a proposition absurd on its face." He continued: "Broadcasters—as citizens and as members of the press—should be able to say what they think without regulatory sanction. If they choose to represent one perspective, so be it. There are plenty of additional perspectives out there."

In June 1987, Congress tried to reimpose the doctrine legislatively, but Reagan courageously vetoed the bill, which had overwhelming bipartisan support. (Many Republicans back then believed in a regulated media; some still do.) "The framers of the First Amendment," the president maintained, going to the core constitutional question, "confident that public debate would be freer and healthier without the kind of interference represented by the 'Fairness Doctrine,' chose to forbid such regulations in the clearest terms: 'Congress shall make no law ... abridging the freedom of speech, or of the press.'"[16]

That the doctrine was chilling to free speech became indisputable after it was gone. As a 1997 study by Thomas Hazlett and David Sosa charted, AM radio, freed from its shackles, suddenly exploded with news programming and political talk shows. Such "informational" broadcasts expanded from 7 percent of all AM programming to 28 percent just eight years after the Fairness Doctrine's demise; on FM, the increase was from 3 percent to 7 percent. Television soon featured lots more news coverage and opinion, too.[17] Today, about 1,500 radio stations feature a talk or news format—and the vast majority broadcast conservative, libertarian, or populist voices, because that's what draws the listeners, eager for an alternative to a liberal mainstream press. Religious radio—much of it Christian, often with a morally conservative cast—also blossomed in the post–Fairness

Doctrine era: nearly 1,000 stations fall under the religious category. Country music is the only radio format more popular than either of these. Reagan's confidence in the market helped create the media cornucopia.

The left wants to rid the world of this menace to correct—that is, liberal—thinking. A congressional attempt to bring back the Fairness Doctrine in 1993, the "Hush Rush" bill, was a reaction to the sudden emergence of Rush Limbaugh and other conservative radio hosts as seismic forces. The bill withered after the Republicans captured Congress the next year, a victory that many claimed Limbaugh had helped bring about.

For a while after their defeat, liberals went searching for their own Rush—beginning with the radio shows of Jim Hightower and Mario Cuomo in the 1990s and reaching a fever pitch with the heavily bankrolled and much-celebrated rollout of Air America in March 2004. But liberals have cratered on radio. Before it declared bankruptcy, Air America's ratings, never impressive, had sunk into oblivion. Its New York City flagship, WLIB, hemorrhaged nearly half its listenership during one ratings period, falling to a pathetic 0.8 share. That's smaller than the all-Caribbean format the network replaced when it first went live—and nowhere near the ratings of conservative heavyweights like Rush Limbaugh and Sean Hannity in the city. And this despite all the free publicity that the network and its top host, the comedian Al Franken, enjoyed in the mainstream press. Of course, it's difficult to generate a decent audience in America when your hosts engage in America-bashing all day long.

So over the last few years, Democratic politicians and activists have begun to talk openly about restoring the Fairness Doctrine. Of course, fairness mandates would force liberal radio to accommodate "the other side," but getting a lot of right-leaning broadcasts off the air would be more than worth the price. The mandates, in fact, would have a twofer effect: they would also curb the sales of conservative books, often snubbed by mainstream media outlets and thus heavily dependent on the conservative talk radio circuit to find readers. "I don't know how else we would reach those buyers, given that most other media, except FOX, of course, are closed to conservatives," says Adam Bellow, an executive editor at HarperCollins.[18]

The plot to resurrect the Fairness Doctrine looks all the more nefarious considering that the left, after being outpaced on the Web initially, has now gained a solid foothold in the blogosphere. As Daniel Henninger of the *Wall Street Journal* explains, "Reimposing the Fairness Doctrine, essentially a toxic cocktail of boredom, would cause a narcotized right-wing base to sit on its hands, handing an advantage in the turnout wars to the (properly) unregulated political organizers of the left-wing Web."[19]

The new "fairness" campaign was kicked off in 2004, when Media Matters for America, a newly formed liberal watchdog linked to George Soros, started an online campaign to encourage Congress to bring back the Fairness Doctrine. "Tired of imbalanced political discourse on our airwaves?" asked David Brock, the head of Media Matters (and an apostate from conservatism). "By restoring a diversity of fact and opinion to programming,

Fairness Doctrine legislation restores a concept that has been lost since the 1980s—that because the public owns the airwaves, the public is entitled to be adequately informed by the broadcasters of news and opinion."[20] The campaign gained little traction at a time when Democrats controlled neither House nor Senate. Yet given that Media Matters had connections not only with Soros "affiliates" like MoveOn.org and the New Democratic Network, but also with the Clintons—John Podesta, formerly Bill Clinton's chief of staff, helped Brock get the group started—its early efforts merited more notice than they received.

House Democrats had already begun to propose bills to restore the Fairness Doctrine. (A remade FCC, with pro-regulation commissioners, could simply impose it.) Rep. Louise Slaughter, a New York Democrat who introduced one of the bills, said that right-ruled radio was a grave threat to American freedoms, "a waste of good broadcast time, and a waste of our airwaves." People "may hear whatever they please and whatever they choose," she told PBS's Bill Moyers, in a statement as incoherent as it was illiberal. "And of course they have the right to turn it off. But that's not good enough either. The fact is that they need the responsibility of the people who are licensed to use our airwaves judiciously and responsibly to call them to account if they don't."

Though radio was their primary target, the Democrats had other media in their sights. When asked by Moyers if she was proposing the new Fairness Doctrine to cover FOX News and MSNBC as well, Slaughter responded: "You bet. . . . Fairness isn't going to hurt anybody."[21] If there's anything liberals hate more than talk radio, it's FOX News, which has dominated cable news by appealing to conservative viewers fed up with the networks' liberal bias. Rep. Maurice Hinchey, another New York Democrat who is promoting a Fairness Doctrine bill, went so far as to host a special Capitol Hill screening of *Outfoxed: Rupert Murdoch's War on Journalism*, a hit job masquerading as a documentary. Slaughter, Hinchey, Bernie Sanders (Vermont), Jay Inslee (Washington State), and several other House leftists have formed the Future of American Media Congress to push for a media crackdown. This agitation remained mostly below the public radar, however.

In 2007, the campaign for a new Fairness Doctrine finally grabbed headlines. Senator James Inhofe of Oklahoma ignited a hullabaloo by noting that he had once overheard Senators Hillary Clinton and Barbara Boxer discussing a "legislative fix" for talk radio. Both Clinton and Boxer denied it, but Senator Dianne Feinstein quickly weighed in, saying on FOX News that talk radio was too "explosive," that it pushed people to "extreme views without a lot of information," and that she was going to look closely into restoring the Fairness Doctrine. John Kerry wasn't so cautious: "I think the Fairness Doctrine ought to be there," he said bluntly on the *Brian Lehrer Show* on WNYC. Conservatives had been able "to squeeze down and squeeze out opinion of opposing views. I think it's been a very important transition in the imbalance of our public eye." According to *The American Spectator*, a senior advisor to House Speaker Nancy Pelosi offered a nakedly political rationale for reinstating the doctrine: "Conservative radio is a huge threat and political advantage for Republicans and we have to find a way to limit it."[22]

A Senate exchange in 2007 between Richard Durbin, Democrat from Illinois (and the number-two-ranking senator), and Norm Coleman, Republican from Minnesota, illuminates the contrasting worldviews in the debate over media "fairness."[23] Senator Durbin opened with a challenge: "What if the marketplace does not provide opportunities to hear both points of view? Since the people who are seeking the licenses are using America's airwaves, does the government, speaking for the people of this country, have any interest at that point to step in and make sure there is . . . a fair and balanced approach to the information given to the American people?"

Senator Coleman would have none of it. "In a time in 1949 when you had three network TV stations, basically, when you had limited channels of communication, I presume there was a legitimate concern on the part of some that, in fact, government needs to step in and ensure balance," he conceded. "But now we're in 2007. We're at a time where we've got 20,000, you know, opportunities for stations and satellite, where you have cable, you have blogs, you have a whole range of information." How could the market *not* be providing "both points of view," given such abundance? Coleman might also have asked: Why "both" points of view? Should government ensure that Islamists get a "fair" hearing? How about communists? Libertarians? Anti-Darwinists? On what principle would regulators differentiate among worldviews, or would all require "fair" treatment?

Then Coleman made the more fundamental—in fact, the decisive—philosophical and constitutional argument: "In the end, consumers also have a right based on the market to make choices. And so if they make choices that say we want to hear more of one side than the other, that's okay. And I think it's very dangerous, I say to my—my friend from Illinois, I think it's very dangerous for government to be in the position of deciding what's fair and balanced." Coleman instructed his fellow solon to look around them. "As we see on the floor of the Senate, oftentimes amongst ourselves, learned—hopefully learned—individuals who've the great, humble opportunity to serve in the U.S. Senate, we often have differences as to what is fair and balanced. And so the reason I think we have a First Amendment is that we get government out of . . . measuring, controlling, dictating, [and] regulating content."

Coleman closed with a potent rhetorical move: "John Kennedy stated, 'We are not afraid to entrust the American people with unpleasant facts, foreign ideas, alien philosophies, and competitive values. For a nation that is afraid to let its people judge the truth and falsehood in an open market is a nation that is afraid of its people.'" (The Kennedy administration didn't always live up to this ideal, as documented by Friendly in *The Good Guys, the Bad Guys, and the First Amendment*.) "I'm not afraid of . . . the people," Coleman said. "I'm not afraid of the people having access to the information, ideas that they want to have access to. But I am afraid of the government stepping in and regulating content. We have a First Amendment. That's the underpinning, the foundation of all the other amendments. The Fairness Doctrine flies in the face of that."

Indeed, as Coleman suggested, even if you believe in regulating the radio dial, the Fairness Doctrine wouldn't be effective in an age of information abundance. Citizens could just "turn the dial" to satellite radio, Internet radio stations, their iPods' menu of podcasts, and so on. And that's just the competition for our ears.

To add yet one more argument to the armory opposing the Fairness Doctrine, there is also something radically unfair and illogical about reviving fairness regulations only for broadcast station operators when they face all this new competition from a new media universe that is (so far) unconstrained.

It's easy to dismiss the Democrats' Orwellian policy prescriptions as unlikely to become law. But with such high-level backing—including that of Al Gore, another leading Democrat who thinks we need to reregulate the airwaves—the prospect is not far-fetched. "Unless broadcasters take steps to voluntarily balance their programming, they can expect a return of fairness rules if Democrats keep control of Congress and win the White House" in 2008, observes Craig Crawford, a political analyst

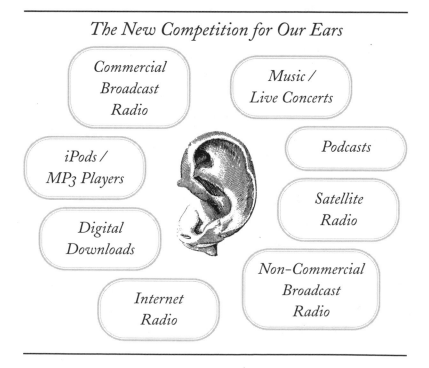

The New Competition for Our Ears

Commercial Broadcast Radio

Music / Live Concerts

iPods / MP3 Players

Podcasts

Digital Downloads

Satellite Radio

Internet Radio

Non-Commercial Broadcast Radio

for *Congressional Quarterly* and NBC.[24] The political scene seems even less reassuring when you consider that support for the Fairness Doctrine isn't limited to Democrats. Back in 1987, a leading Republican, Senator Trent Lott, tried to save the doctrine when the Reagan administration got rid of it. "Heaven knows what would happen without a Fairness Doctrine," he warned. And after the 2007 immigration bill went down to defeat, Lott denounced talk radio for "running the country." Incumbent politicians often find it hard to come to the defense of institutions that might amplify the voices of their critics (as Chapter Five, on campaign-finance regulations, will confirm).

Many Americans don't realize that most countries regulate their media far more extensively than the United States does (and that's why nothing like American political talk radio exists elsewhere). European Union advisory bodies have even kicked around a fairness rule for the Internet, which would force all opinion sites viewable in Europe—from tiny blogs to big news organizations—to post opposing views or face fines.[25] That idea has gained some traction here in the States, as we saw with Cass Sunstein's proposal for "electronic sidewalks," on which partisan websites would have to carry links to opposing views. Freedom-minded FCC Commissioner Robert McDowell warned that a new Fairness Doctrine could easily extend to political websites.[26] (More on the threat to a free Internet in the next chapter.)

The push for "fairness" would be unlikely to stop with equal-time rules, observes John Fund in the *Wall Street Journal*. "Al Franken, the liberal former Air America host who is now running for the Senate in Minnesota, is already slipping into the role of potential legislative censor of his old industry," Fund writes. Early in 2007, Franken declared, "You shouldn't be able to lie on the air. You can't utter obscenities in a broadcast, so why should you be able to lie? You should be fined for lying."[27] But who decides what is a lie?

Consider in this light a 2007 study on talk radio from the Center for American Progress, a liberal think tank founded by John Podesta. Contending that the popularity of conservative voices on the airwaves results not from listener preferences but instead from a "structural imbalance" in the marketplace that has meant too much big corporate control of radio, the study proposed correcting that imbalance (and getting more liberals on the air) by tightening ownership regulations and ensuring "greater local accountability over radio licensing." This proposal would guarantee lots more government meddling in the radio marketplace, by local officials, among others. But the most preposterous element of CAP's regulatory agenda was the requirement that commercial radio owners "who fail to abide by enforceable public interest obligations" (whatever that means) would have to pay a penalty, which would go toward public broadcasting. Thus not only would radio operators—struggling already against many new media competitors—find themselves tangled in a thicket of new content regulations; they would also face the threat of having to bankroll their publicly owned competitors on NPR.[28] This is just a sneaky version of a new Fairness Doctrine, making the ominous proposal by the Democratic presidential nominee Barack Obama to "clarify the public interest obligations of broadcasters who occupy the nation's spectrum" all the more troubling.[29]

And can we trust the Supreme Court to defend free speech and block any new Fairness Doctrine by reversing *Red Lion v. FCC* once and for all? The newest justices on the bench,

John Roberts and Samuel Alito, have shown admirable First Amendment sensitivity, as have Clarence Thomas and Antonin Scalia. But others on the divided court are far less reliable. This is, after all, a court that couldn't muster five votes to block something as blatantly unconstitutional and speech-restricting as modern campaign-finance regulations.

Nor is it obvious how the politics of "fairness" would play out with the public. A Rasmussen poll in 2008 found 47 percent of those polled supporting the idea of requiring radio and television stations to offer "equal amounts of conservative and liberal political commentary," and 39 percent opposed, while 31 percent wanted the government to regulate websites for political content. Rasmussen found that liberals support a Fairness Doctrine by a margin of 54 percent to 26 percent, while Republicans and unaffiliated voters were more evenly divided. The language of "fairness" is clearly beguiling.[30]

To get a sense of what Democrats really mean by "fairness," though, consider the reason that Durbin and Coleman were sparring. The Republican senator had tried to offer an amendment to a bill that would have banned the FCC from reinstituting the Fairness Doctrine by regulatory fiat. Rather than let the measure be debated by the entire Senate, however, Democratic legislators blocked it from reaching the floor. If the Democrats get a lock on Washington, nothing would please them more than to drag the country back to the good old days, when they didn't have to put up with Rush Limbaugh and Laura Ingraham and countless other conservative voices recasting our public debate.

CHAPTER THREE

NETWORK SOCIALISM

THE LEFT'S CRUSADE to regulate media unfortunately isn't limited to analogue-era prey. A new target is sitting in its cross-hairs: the Internet. Over the past few years, many of the same policymakers and activists who have long trumpeted the Fairness Doctrine have advocated that its rough equivalent apply to Internet service providers. And they've come up with another Orwellian term for the idea: "net neutrality."

Even as telecom, cable, and wireless networks have evolved (and grown fiercely competitive), their operators face dramatic new challenges. The traffic moving across wired and wireless networks is like nothing seen before. YouTube videos, high-def movie downloads, online gaming, massive BitTorrent file transfers, and much more now threaten to clog the Internet. The traffic growth is exponential: "The U.S. Internet of 2015 will be at least 50 times larger than it was in 2006," say George Gilder of the Discovery Institute and Bret Swanson of the Progress & Freedom Foundation.[1] Broadband firms, freed by recent Supreme Court and FCC rulings, want to manage more actively all the data now pulsing through their "pipes"—their cables, fiber optics, phone lines, or wireless connections—offering, for instance, new ultrafast delivery for sites or users willing to pay extra, just as FedEx accelerates delivery of packages for a fee. They might also offer additional services, such as online video or telephony, as part of the package.

But net-neutrality regulation would ban these companies from treating some bits of online traffic or communications more favorably than others, whether for economic or political purposes. Net-neutrality advocates claim that such private efforts to manage high-speed networks—violating the "first-come, first-served" common-carriage principle that governed the old monopolistic Bell System—amount to "digital discrimination." With fanciful rhetoric akin to the language used to promote the Fairness Doctrine, they say that neutrality regulations will "save the Internet" from the "broadband barons," apparently hell-bent on controlling us. Unsurprisingly, the same cast of characters that promotes a Fairness Doctrine—Barack Obama, Hillary Clinton, MoveOn.org, Free Press, the *New York Times*—is orchestrating this new regulatory drive.

Senator Clinton, for example, says that government must mandate neutrality because "each day on the Internet views are discussed and debated in an open forum without fear of censorship or reprisal"—and private companies apparently can't be trusted to keep the Web open. This shows real chutzpah. Anyone who follows media policy closely knows that Clinton's name frequently pops up in news stories about government efforts to regulate old and new media alike. In the early 1990s, for example, she promoted the Children's Television Act, a law that imposed programming requirements and advertising restrictions on television broadcasters. In the mid-nineties, she

45

stood with her husband in support of the Communications Decency Act, which proposed a federal regulatory regime for online speech. She has also sponsored legislation that would have the federal government regulate video games. And don't forget what she said after the Monica Lewinsky scandal erupted back in 1998: "We are all going to have to rethink how we deal with [the Internet], because there are all these competing values. Without any kind of editing function or gatekeeping function, what does it mean to have the right to defend your reputation?"[2] It doesn't seem to be the private sector that is threatening media freedom here.

It may be that with net neutrality, Hillary thinks she has found the "gatekeeping" solution she seeks. It's not hard to imagine a net-neutrality law as the first step toward a Web Fairness Doctrine, with government trying to micromanage networks so as to guarantee "equal treatment" of opposing viewpoints (read: putting pesky reporters like Matt Drudge and all those noisy right-wing bloggers back in their place).

It's a brilliant tactic. Why exert all your energy attempting to reimpose "fairness" on broadcasters alone when you can capture them—and much more—by regulating the entire Internet? After all, in a world of media convergence and abundance, the bright lines that once separated distinct media sectors have vanished. Everything from TV shows to text messages runs on multiple networks, making the old, broadcast-oriented Fairness Doctrine a less effective means of reestablishing a liberal media monopoly. Net neutrality could be the backdoor way to get regulatory oversight of the entire media marketplace.

In practice, net neutrality would be anything but fair or neutral. For starters, the problem it addresses is nonexistent.

Network owners don't want to restrict the flow of speech; they want more of it—not for any high-minded social purpose but because more traffic equals more revenue. "The providers have no incentive to kick anybody out," notes Gilder. "They want to get as much content as possible on their conduit. That's what attracts customers."[3] No network provider ever got rich restricting the flow of goods or services over its own system.

Further, the "discrimination" that net-neutrality advocates aim to make illegal consists of routine practices that all network operators use to balance traffic loads and make their systems run smoothly and efficiently. For example, how can an operator ease network congestion caused by high-bandwidth traffic hogs? It can delay the hogs' traffic while other traffic gets through. Or it can use traditional pricing techniques such as express-lane premiums or metered pricing to charge by the minute or the amount of bandwidth gobbled up. These are indeed forms of "network discrimination"; but it's the sort of discrimination that is essential to ensure that other network users are treated fairly. Not every broadband customer is a bandwidth glutton. Many users only Web-surf casually, check e-mail, and maybe upload photos of the kids once in a while. The network manager's job is to keep those customers happy—and get more folks like them to sign up. This may require tailored pricing or limiting certain users' excessive use of the network so that millions of routine Web-surfers don't have their experience degraded by the hogs.

If broadband network owners aren't allowed to engage in such rational business practices, heavy bandwidth users will benefit at the expense of lighter users. There's nothing nondiscriminatory about that, observes Harry Alford Jr., president and CEO of the National Black Chamber of Commerce: "One of the most serious threats to widespread broadband adoption, particularly for minorities in America, is unbridled peer-to-peer activity that will sop up the majority of available bandwidth, raise prices for internet access and dampen the pace of investments of new networks in underserved communities." Similarly, Jose Marquez, president and CEO of the Latinos in Information Sciences and Technology Association, points to the hypocrisy of net-neutrality champions: "These self-styled champions of 'equality' are actually defending the right of a minority of big users who clog the Internet for everyone else. That sounds like 'net inequality' to me."[4]

The response by net-neutrality advocates—especially the bandwidth hogs—is predictable: "Just give us more capacity!" And that reveals both the ignorance and the hubris of the neutrality movement. It's easy to say that networks should be bigger, better, and faster. But broadband doesn't just fall from the sky like manna. Expanding network capacity takes a considerable investment of money, and making those investments is a business, not a charity. Carriers must recoup their up-front costs if they are to keep innovating, investing, and growing. There's no way for them to do it without balancing costs and managing existing networks to a degree. Some carriers may provide the equivalent of "one-stop shopping," argues Christopher Yoo, a law professor at Vanderbilt, while others may target niche markets to become like "specialty stores"—emphasizing Internet telephony, for instance, or beefing up security features.[5] Such product differentiation would be impossible under neutrality regulation.

Luckily, most networks currently remain free of innovation-killing regulation, and serious investment in capacity expansion is now going on. But nothing guarantees that the investment will pan out. Consider telecom giant Verizon's on-going rollout of its multibillion-dollar fiber-optic service (FIOS). The company aims to establish state-of-the-art fiber links in every neighborhood. Many industry observers, though, have serious doubts about Verizon's chances of profiting from this expensive gambit. Craig Moffett, a media and communications analyst with Bernstein Research, estimates that FIOS costs Verizon roughly $4,000 to $5,000 per home connected. Verizon crews must spend hours, sometimes days, at each home to get subscribers up and running. But those subscribers might not stick with Verizon once the installation is complete. In order to stay competitive, cable operators have been slashing prices and luring customers in most neighborhoods where Verizon deploys FIOS. Verizon's experiment could work if subscriber rolls grow and costs fall. But if regulation creates more financial uncertainty or market instability, the ambitious investment effort is far likelier to fizzle.

Net-neutrality utopians remain oblivious to such real-world business concerns. For them, the broadband marketplace is one big commons or public good. Regulations that keep network owners from pricing and managing their networks as they see fit —networks they have built with their own money, after all—tell them, in effect: "Your networks are yours in name only. The larger community of Internet users, through the FCC or other regu-latory bodies, will set the parameters of how your infrastructure gets used." Why would a network operator or potential opera-tor invest another penny of risk capital under these conditions?

At the root of such infrastructure socialism is a static worldview. Neutrality advocates want to micromanage the existing system, ignoring the implications for current networks and for the development of future ones. They see an existing platform —a telephone network, a cable or wireless system—and think it should be theirs for the taking. This reflects a typical liberal redistributionist mind-set, and it's a recipe for technological stasis. Ours is a wildly innovative, creative culture: new communications technologies have transformed our lives for the better and will continue to do so, but only if creators believe that they can reap the fruits of their labor.

Instead of fixating on maximizing consumer welfare within the confines of existing systems, net-neutrality proponents need to think about how the networks of the future will get funded and built. Well-heeled Silicon Valley companies like Google and Amazon (misguidedly) support neutrality because they don't want to pay more for bandwidth, which they would probably have to do in a non-neutral regime in order to keep up with the competition. But transforming broadband into a kind of lackluster public utility won't create the networks of the future; it's much more likely to result in a big Internet slowdown.

Neutrality evangelists also ignore the many potential unintended consequences of regulation. For one, net neutrality would swiftly generate mountains of regulation and litigation. Neutrality regulation "is great news for all the telecom lawyers (like me) who get paid far too much to make sense out of idiotic new laws like this one," writes Peter Huber. The advocates, he says, claim that "a simple two-word law is all we really need— an equal rights amendment for bits" to achieve Internet nirvana.

In reality, "It will be a 2 million-word law by the time Congress, the Federal Communications Commission and the courts are done with it. Grand principles always end up as spaghetti in this industry, because they aim to regulate networks that are far more complicated than anything you have ever seen heaped up beside an amusing little glass of Chianti," Huber observes.[6]

You simply can't put something as amorphous as a "digital nondiscrimination" mandate on the books and then expect that regulators *won't* abuse it—and that means competing teams of lawyers, consultants, and economists trying to figure out all the regulators' decisions. Anyone who followed the legal skirmishes surrounding the implementation of the Telecommunications Act of 1996 will understand the point. Generally viewed as a deregulatory statute, the act contained some fuzzy language on how the FCC should determine the "cost" of various network elements, such as wires and switches, that telecom operators were required to share with competitors. You might ask: How much legal wrangling could there be over defining a tiny word like "cost"? Well, here's a quick tally of the paperwork that the FCC produced in just three major "competition" rules, struggling to define the "cost" of unbundled network elements:

- Local Competition Order (1996): 737 pages, 3,283 footnotes
- UNE Remand Order (1999): 262 pages, 1,040 footnotes
- UNE Triennial Review (2003): 576 pages, 2,447 footnotes

That's 1,575 pages and 6,770 footnotes' worth of regulation in just three orders—not counting the dozens of other rules and clarifications that the FCC issued to implement other parts of the Telecom Act. Nor does the tally include the hundreds of additional rules issued by state public utility commissions. And this was the aftermath of a bill that was supposed to be deregulatory.

But wait; it gets worse. The page count doesn't even begin to cover the tens of thousands of pages of legal filings, economic studies, consultant reports, and other documents submitted to the FCC and state agencies by groups and individuals looking to have a say in the matter. The lawyers indeed cleaned up, just as they would under neutrality mandates. Greg Sidak of Georgetown University Law School found that the number of telecom lawyers—as measured by membership in the Federal Communications Bar Association—grew by a stunning 73 percent during the late 1990s. That was largely driven by a 37 percent hike in FCC spending and a tripling of the number of pages of regulations in the FCC Record in the post–Telecom Act period. Sidak argues, "If one assumes (very conservatively) that the average income of an American telecommunications lawyer is $100,000, then the current membership of the FCBA represents an annual expenditure on legal services of at least $340 million."[7] Following one controversial FCC rulemaking in 2003, Dana Frix, a telecom lawyer with Chadbourne & Parke, told the *New York Times*, "Every word will be challenged. . . . My children will go to college on this stuff. This is a lawyer's dream."[8]

The net-neutrality crowd ignores this dismal track record and pretends that this time around, "the people" will call the shots at the FCC. History tells a different story: one of "regulatory capture" by inside-the-Beltway interests. "Because regulatory commissions are of necessity intimately involved in the affairs of a particular industry," notes Judge Richard Posner, "the regulators and their staffs are exposed to strong interest group pressures."[9] Long ago, in the seminal *Economics of Regulation*, Alfred Kahn pointed out that the regulatory commission that is responsible for "the continued provision and improvement of service" will come "increasingly and understandably to identify the interest of the public with that of the existing companies on whom it must rely to deliver goods."[10] These days, it is hardly remarkable to think of regulation in such terms, as news reports are replete with tales of how various special-interest groups attempt to "game" the regulatory process in their favor. Net-neutrality regulation would certainly not be immune from such pressures.

Net neutrality's corporate champions fail to realize that there's no guarantee that the quest for neutrality would stop at infrastructure providers. Why not "search engine neutrality," too? The educational site KinderStart slapped a lawsuit on Google in 2006 for downgrading its page rank; the suit argued that Google had become an "essential facility" and thus should face government review for fairness. Though the case was eventually dismissed, the arguments made against Google's freedom to run its business are analogous to those that Google is now making against the telecom, cable, and wireless network providers. Google would be wise to remember that in the world of regulation, what goes around often comes around.

That many liberals would support net neutrality is no surprise—they have long favored government regulation of media and communications markets (and much else). What's shocking, however, is that some conservative and family groups have joined forces with them. The Parents Television Council and Gun Owners of America, for example, have thrown their support behind this Big Government crusade.

In the most unholy of these alliances, Roberta Combs, president of the Christian Coalition of America, and Nancy Keenan, president of NARAL Pro-Choice America, wrote a *Washington Post* op-ed in October 2007 calling for a congressional investigation of purported "censorship" by wired and wireless operators.[11] They claimed that private companies were seeking to muffle speech over the networks. "We're asking Congress to convene hearings on whether existing law is sufficient to guarantee the free flow of information and to protect against corporate censorship," Combs and Keenan wrote.

Prompting their call for regulation was a September 2007 incident in which Verizon Wireless blocked text messages from NARAL, deeming them "controversial." Verizon admitted that it had made a mistake and immediately changed its policy. But NARAL and the Christian Coalition claimed that the incident showed why government-enforced neutrality was essential. In reality, the incident proved the opposite: the message got out. In fact, NARAL has probably never had such great press; the blogosphere in particular was all over the story.

Here, sunlight proved the best disinfectant: press attention and public pressure changed corporate behavior. Even if it hadn't, plenty of other carriers and media providers would have been all too happy to deliver NARAL's message. In a world of abundant media options and outlets, Verizon would have no practical ability to "censor" speech even if it wanted to.

Unsurprisingly, the editors of the *New York Times*, guardians of sacred liberal causes, disagreed. Like N A R A L and the Christian Coalition, the *Times* sensed a corporate conspiracy to stifle dissent, and in an over-the-top editorial suggested that Verizon's mistake constituted "textbook censorship." "Any government that tried it would be rightly labeled authoritarian," the *Times* argued, and "the First Amendment prohibits the United States government from anything approaching that sort of restriction."[12]

The editorial writers at the *Times* apparently need to brush up on the First Amendment. It's certainly true that any government action restricting online speech in this fashion would be unconstitutional. But a world of difference exists between state censorship and a private company's exercising editorial discretion to transmit—or not transmit—certain messages or types of content. As the Framers understood, when government censors, it does so sweepingly (prohibiting the public, at least in theory, from seeing or hearing what it disapproves of) and coercively (punishing those who evade the restrictions with fines, penalties, or even jail time). Not so for Verizon, or any other private carrier, which has no power to censor in a sweeping and coercive fashion.

Professor Laurence Tribe of Harvard Law School made this point eloquently at a Progress & Freedom Foundation event in 2 0 0 7. In his view, further, those who would impose net-neutrality regulations on First Amendment grounds fail to appreciate "the fundamental right of editorial discretion. For the government to tell that entity that it cannot exercise that right in a certain way, that it must allow the projection of what it doesn't want to include, is a violation of its First Amendment rights."[13] The principle that Tribe articulated would apply equally to the editors of the *New York Times* if they decided, say, not to run an advertisement from the Ku Klux Klan. That's why it's puzzling that the *Times* ended its Verizon editorial by arguing that "freedom of speech must be guaranteed, right now, in a digital world just as it has been protected in a world of paper and ink." Does the editorialist believe, then, that government should regulate what ads the *Times* may run in its own pages?

The Christian Coalition's support for mandated neutrality is particularly misguided. A new Fairness Doctrine for the Internet would have the same chilling effect on the vibrant exchange of ideas—especially conservative ideas—that the old Fairness Doctrine did for broadcast TV and radio. The Christian Coalition and other conservative and family groups have been major beneficiaries of the modern, unregulated media marketplace, which has allowed conservatives to spread their message to a much broader audience. If they help bring about a neutrality regime, they'll have only themselves to blame when, one day, the feds come knocking, requiring them to ensure more "fairness" on their websites or in their e-mail communications.

Many battles have already been fought over net neutrality, and more are coming. Thanks primarily to Republican efforts last year, both the House and (narrowly) the Senate fought back a push to make net neutrality the new central directive in cyberspace. But new proposals popped up as quickly as legislators beat down older ones. Rep. Ed Markey, Democrat of Massachusetts, has introduced legislation in 2008—the perversely titled

"Internet Freedom Preservation Act"—that would require the FCC to study the issue in more detail.

In fact, the FCC has already started looking at it. In early 2008, the agency opened an investigation into network management policies, focusing on how the cable operator Comcast was dealing with BitTorrent traffic. Some of the most vociferous net-neutrality advocates, including Free Press, organizer of a "Save the Internet" campaign, once again bombarded the FCC with online petitions. The activists also agitated relentlessly for more "town hall meetings" to allow "the people"—a few hundred MoveOn.org or Free Press operatives, that is—to vent their harebrained theories about corporate conspiracy. Markey was all too eager to oblige in his bill, calling for eight "public broadband summits" across America in the year following its passage. And in August, the FCC ruled that Comcast "unduly interfered" with Internet users' "right to assess the lawful Internet content and to use the applications of their choice," taking a big step toward making net neutrality mandatory.

So this high-tech holy war will continue. But the left's goal is the same as ever: to get hold of modern media infrastructure and outlets in order to force a liberal worldview on all of us. If they succeed in placing net-neutrality mandates on the books, we'll all be forced to be "fair," which sounds a lot like being forced to be free.

The left's impulse to regulate and control media isn't just about establishing a media world congenial to its favored political opinions. It also manifests itself, as the next chapter shows, in a fear of the (purportedly) corrupting influence of new media and a belief that government can save us from that influence. Here, the Nanny State liberals get some help from conservatives.

CHAPTER FOUR

NEOPHOBIA

NEW MEDIA have always met with suspicion. From the waltz to rock-and-roll to rap music, from movies to comic books to video games, from radio and television to the Internet and social networking websites—every new media format or technology spawns a fresh debate about the potential negative effects it might have on society, and especially on children.[1] *The Economist* has editorialized about "the neophobia that has pitted the old against the entertainment of the young for centuries," noting that it actually dates from antiquity, with Plato's argument in the *Phædrus* that the relatively newfangled medium of writing corrupted the memory-building powers of oral culture.[2]

Of course, sometimes new media *can* create new challenges or problems with which society must grapple. Yet the critics of video games, the expanded world of cable and satellite TV, social networking sites, and so on are often conjuring up threats where none exist, while ignoring the positive benefits that many of today's new media options offer us.

* * *

Neophobia

Video games are a particularly worrisome new problem for many lawmakers, who fear that the industry—with receipts now topping those of the Hollywood box office—threatens to transform our kids into drooling zombies or raging sociopaths. Plenty of Republicans have a beef with the medium, but congressional Democrats are increasingly leading the crusade to regulate it. For example, in 2005, Senators Hillary Clinton, Joe Lieberman, and Evan Bayh introduced the Family Entertainment Protection Act, which proposed a federal regulatory regime for video games. Though it didn't pass, the measure would have granted the Federal Trade Commission authority to regulate the sale of games and the ratings now imposed voluntarily by the industry.

Vulgar, blood-soaked video games are precipitating a "silent epidemic" of media desensitization, Clinton says, and "stealing the innocence of our children."[3] And if we are to believe Senator Clinton and her colleagues, parents have no power over the video games their kids play, so federal bureaucrats therefore must act *in loco parentis*. In Clintonian terms: it takes a village to raise a responsible gamer. But this argument doesn't hold water. Parents have plenty of tools and methods available to select what's best for their children.

For starters, just think about the cost of video games. Most new titles retail for $30 to $60, and the consoles to play them on run over $300. Most kids don't have that kind of cash on hand. Thus, parents can exercise the ultimate parental-control tool: the power of the purse.

Parents also have access to a great deal of information about games before they buy them for their kids. The video game industry has developed a content rating and labeling system that is the most sophisticated, descriptive, and effective ratings system ever devised by any major media sector in America. The Entertainment Software Rating Board (ESRB), established in 1994, is a self-regulatory rating and labeling body that rates over a thousand games per year. Virtually every title produced by major game developers for retail sale today carries one of seven ESRB ratings and several of over thirty content "descriptors." (Generally speaking, the only games without ESRB ratings are those developed by amateurs that are freely traded or down-loaded via the Internet.) By glancing at the back of a game container, parents can quickly gauge the title's appropriateness. So *Grand Theft Auto IV*, with an "M" rating (for "mature") fea-tures Blood, Intense Violence, Partial Nudity, Strong Lan-guage, Strong Sexual Content, and Use of Drugs and Alcohol. That one's not for little Johnny. Plus, ESRB's website enables parents, before they even get to Game Stop, to enter the name of any game and retrieve its rating and content descriptors. Surveys show that most parents find the ratings and labels very helpful. Studies by Peter D. Hart Research Associates reveal that 89 percent of parents of children who play video games are aware of the ESRB ratings and that 85 percent consult them regularly when buying games for their families.[4]

Parents wishing to verify ESRB game ratings, or who just want to know more about what's in the games, have many inde-pendent options. Organizations such as Common Sense Media, What They Play, Gamer Dad, Children's Technology Review, and MediaWise "KidScore" have websites filled with detailed game reviews and descriptions of game content.[5] And user-generated reviews on sites like Amazon and Metacritic feature excellent product summaries, often written by parents. Think of all these sites and services as a voluntary village that can help

ESRB Ratings: Parental Awareness & Use

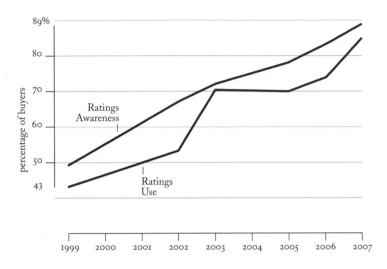

Source: Entertainment Software Ratings Board, Peter D. Hart Research Associates

us raise our children, as opposed to Hillary's top-down, bureaucrat-run vision.

Once parents bring games home, they have still more ways to control gaming activities. Every new gaming console and PC operating system comes equipped with sophisticated tools that allow parents to block games based on their ESRB ratings. Newer consoles let parents prevent online gaming, chat, downloads, and purchases. Alternatively, parents can say yes to online gaming for their kids but restrict it to preapproved "buddy lists," such as other neighborhood children or school friends. In November 2007, Microsoft announced that it was also offering Xbox 360 owners a downloadable "Family Timer" feature, which lets parents limit how and when children play games on the console.[6]

And many parents also establish household rules to limit gaming, of course. A 2007 Pew Internet & American Life

Project survey found that 59 percent of parents limit gaming time.[7] Many parents insist, too, that their kids play video games only in open areas where they can be watched. In sum, most parents are parenting, and they don't need the Democrats—or anyone in Congress—to help them raise their kids.

Critics will retort: the government still needs to get involved because all these video games are just too violent or racy; it's an unprecedented situation. But that's another myth. The vast majority of video games sold today are fine for young children. In 2007, for example, almost 75 percent of all ESRB-rated games got either an "E" rating (for "Everyone") or an "E 10+" (for "Everyone 10 and older").

Sure, some popular titles, like the *Grand Theft Auto* series and *Resident Evil*, contain plenty of gruesome violence and unsavory language, but they're clearly labeled and easily blocked.

ESRB Ratings Breakdown by Year

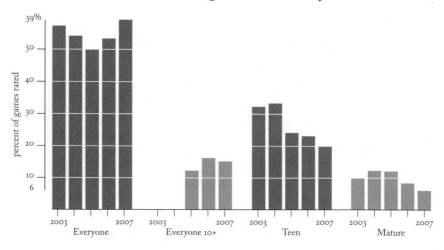

Source: Entertainment Software Rating Board
Note: The "E-10+" rating designation was added in 2005.

Moreover, there are offensive books out there, too—including manuals about building bombs and how to murder your wife. Why, then, aren't Senator Clinton and friends proposing a federal regulatory regime for books? After all, books not only lack any sort of rating system; they are also readily available in public libraries.

Some parents say they have their own children's gaming habits under control, but they are concerned about what happens when Junior visits Johnny's house down the street. This problem, too, is nothing new, however; parents have always had to deal with negligent neighbors. The best solution is for Junior's parents to talk with Johnny's parents about what constitutes acceptable entertainment when their children visit one another.

Many parents worry about the effect of violent video games on their kids' sensibilities and behavior. But there's no hard evidence that spending a lot of time offing enemies thrown at him by *Call of Duty IV* will make your thirteen year-old want to try homicide in real life. The most comprehensive study yet on the social effects of such kill-or-be-killed games, conducted by researchers at the University of Illinois and the University of Michigan, found that prolonged playing of *Asheron's Call 2*—a gory online multiplayer fantasy—didn't make study participants more belligerent.[8] It's worth noting that the emergence of video games as a major youth enthusiasm coincided with a striking drop in juvenile violence.

Though the critics' language is positively apocalyptic on this point, the notion that video games reflect a new, inordinate societal preoccupation with violent entertainment is one more legend. In his book *Savage Pastimes: A Cultural History of Violent Entertainment*, Harold Schechter meticulously documents the prevalence of violent fare throughout the history of art and popular entertainment. "Even the most vehement critics of contemporary popular culture would be hard-pressed to find anything in today's mainstream mass entertainment as alarming as the gore-drenched, gun-worshipping fantasies that [Mickey] Spillane and his publisher dished out for the delectation of millions of ordinary American readers in the supposedly halcyon days of the 1950s," argues Schechter.[9] He also mentions the extraordinary gore of "pulp" comics during that decade. And the top-rated television program of 1954, Disney's *Davy Crockett*, "contained a staggering amount of graphic violence," including scalpings, stabbings, "brainings," hatchet and tomahawk blows, and more. The series finale took place at the Alamo and boasted, says Schechter, a "level of carnage [that] remains unsurpassed in the history of televised children's entertainment."[10] What's more, the show aired Wednesday nights at 7:30 to target the elementary school viewership.

In a 2001 circuit court decision, Judge Richard Posner addressed the purported dangers of video violence in a blistering, tour-de-force opinion that included a review of violence in literature throughout history.[11] "Self-defense, protection of others, dread of the 'undead,' fighting against overwhelming odds—these are all age-old themes of literature, and ones particularly appealing to the young," he noted. "To shield children right up to the age of 18 from exposure to violent descriptions and images would not only be quixotic, but deforming; it would leave them unequipped to cope with the world as we know it. People are unlikely to become well-functioning, independent-minded adults and responsible citizens if they are raised in an intellectual bubble."

Many people, including many children, clearly have a desire to see *depictions* of violence. They might even imagine themselves to be role-playing or living out fantasies in the imaginary worlds created by authors, television and radio writers and entertainers, and now video game developers. One need only read the works of Shakespeare to realize that this instinct is deeply ingrained in the human psyche. How many knives have been plunged into how many backs during the countless performances of Shakespeare's most revered works over the past five centuries? Some of his plays—*King Lear*, *Macbeth*, and *Titus Andronicus*, in particular—contain scenes of extreme violence, murder, and even mutilation. Yet Shakespeare's works are available in every library and school in America, and rightly so.

Could it be that violent entertainment might even have some beneficial effects? From the Bible to *Beowulf* to Batman, depictions of violence have been used not only to teach moral lessons, but also to allow people— including children—to engage in a kind of escapism that can have a therapeutic effect on the human psyche. Aristotle used the term *katharsis* when discussing the importance of Greek tragedies, which often contained violence. He suggested that these tragedies helped the audience, "through pity and fear effecting the proper purgation of these emotions."[12] Aristotle spoke highly of tragedies that used provocative or titillating storytelling to its fullest effect:

> Tragedy is an imitation not only of a complete action, but of events inspiring fear or pity. Such an effect is best produced when the events come on us by surprise; and the effect is heightened when, at the same time, they follow as cause and effect. The tragic wonder will then be

greater than if they happened of themselves or by accident; for even coincidences are most striking when they have an air of design. We may instance the statue of Mitys at Argos, which fell upon his murderer while he was a spectator at a festival, and killed him. Such events seem not to be due to mere chance. Plots, therefore, constructed on these principles are necessarily the best.[13]

What Aristotle believed important about such tales was precisely that they give rise to a heightened sense of "tragic wonder" that helps us purge away or balance out similar passions brewing within us.[14]

One could just as easily apply this thinking to many of the most popular video games that children play today, including those with violent overtones. Here's Gerard Jones, in his book *Killing Monsters: Why Children Need Fantasy, Super Heroes, and Make-Believe Violence*:

> One of the functions of stories and games is to help children rehearse for what they'll be in later life. Anthropologists and psychologists who study play, however, have shown that there are many other functions as well—one of which is to enable children to pretend to be just what they know they'll *never* be. Exploring, in a safe and controlled context, what is impossible or too dangerous or forbidden to them is a crucial tool in accepting the limits of reality. Playing with rage is a valuable way to reduce its power. Being evil and destructive in imagination is a vital compensation for the wildness we all have to surrender on our way to being good people.[15]

Neophobia

Steven Johnson's *Everything Bad Is Good for You: How Today's Popular Culture Is Actually Making Us Smarter* presents another argument for looking at video games in a favorable —or at least not unfavorable—light. Johnson contends that video games are growing increasingly sophisticated, providing players a "cognitive workout" far more stimulating, rewarding, and even educational than much of the media content they were force-fed in the past.[16] (Admittedly, one might spend one's time more usefully by reading, say, Michael Chabon's new novel.) Modern games, including those with violent content, require children to analyze complex social networks, manage resources, track subtle narrative intertwining, and recognize long-term patterns.[17] James Paul Gee, a professor of reading at the University of Wisconsin's school of education, makes a comparable argument in *What Video Games Have to Teach Us about Learning and Literacy.*[18]

A growing number of innovators recognize the intellectual benefits of gaming and seek to use video games for educational and therapeutic purposes. The Serious Games Initiative got its start in 2002, when the U.S. Army released *America's Army*, a free online game that allows players to "live" the army. More than 5 million people have registered to play, reported *USA Today*.[19] Venture capital and philanthropic dollars are pouring into Serious Games projects in health care, mathematics, and government and corporate training. One encouraging early result has been *Free Dive*, a game that distracts children suffering from chronic pain or undergoing painful operations in real life with a calming underwater virtual reality.[20]

Such thinking will undoubtedly remain controversial, perhaps even outlandish to some. But art and entertainment have always drawn their share of controversy. Indeed, one generation's trash often becomes a subsequent generation's treasure. Sculptures, paintings, and works of literature widely condemned in one period are often praised and even considered mainstream in the next.[21]

Video games, too, are likely to remain a target of scorn because of a misplaced fear of the new and unknown.[22] In another generation or two, however, society probably will be far more comfortable with the medium, which, if left to flourish, will grow ever more sophisticated. In the short term, the challenge is to ensure that government doesn't act on its worst tendencies by seeking to stifle history's latest form of storytelling. Critics would do better to drop the jeremiads and pick up a joystick. Video games have the potential to be popular culture at its best.

Politicians have also been going after cable and satellite television—a slightly older "new medium"—on content-based grounds. Some policymakers, seeking to clean up cable's supposed excesses, are advocating both direct and indirect forms of content regulation for the subscription TV services offered by cable, satellite, and telecommunications providers.

In 2005, for example, Senators Jay Rockefeller and Kay Bailey Hutchison introduced the "Indecent and Gratuitous and Excessively Violent Programming Control Act," which proposed the regulation of smutty or "excessively violent" shows on pay TV.[23] Most lawmakers, however, realize that such a move would face an immediate—and likely successful—constitutional challenge, since the traditional broadcast-era regulatory rationales don't work for pay TV. One of these is media "scarcity," which would hold that we shouldn't devote part of a very limited medium to indecent programming. But this is now a laughable proposition, as we've seen.

"Pervasiveness" has been the other rationale undergirding traditional broadcast regulation. The notion that radio and TV were "intruders" into the home and "uniquely accessible to children" became the *raison d'être* for FCC content regulation following the Supreme Court's famous *Pacifica* decision in 1978.[24] But that logic is now moot, too. In a new world of media abundance, technological convergence, and cross-platform media flows, nothing is "uniquely accessible." There are countless media outlets and technologies vying for our increasingly fragmented attention spans. And considering that families spend good money—at least $60 per month for basic service—to subscribe to cable or satellite programming, it is impossible to claim that those services represent "intruders" into the home; they are more like invited (if occasionally unruly) guests.

Just as with video games, moreover, parents can easily restrict the television programming that their children consume, relying on tools such as various content rating and labeling systems, the V-Chip, set-top box controls, and other options. The tools let parents tailor media content and consumption to their family's specific needs and values. As the Federal Communications Commission noted in a recent report about the video marketplace, "through the use of advanced set-top boxes and digital video recorders, and the introduction of new mobile video services, consumers are now able to maintain more control over what, when, and how they receive information."[25] If certain parents believe that their children should be raised solely on reruns of *Sesame Street* and *Leave It to Beaver*, these new media technologies can make it happen.

But there's no need to settle for a few classics. While broadcast TV gave families a limited number of children's programs in the past, today they have a broad and growing range of options. Here is a partial list:

Family & Children's Programming Options on Cable, Telco, and Satellite TV

American Life TV
Animal Planet
Anime Network
ABC Family
Black Family Channel
Boomerang
Cartoon Network
Discovery Kids
Disney Channel
Familyland Television Network
Family Net
FUNimation
GAS
Hallmark Channel
Hallmark Movie Channel

HBO Family
KTV-Kids & Teens Television
Nickelodeon
Nick 2
Nick Toons
Noggin (2–5 years)
The N Channel (9–14 years)
PBS Kids Sprout
Showtime Family Zone
Starz! Kids & Family
Toon Disney
Varsity TV
WAM

Source: Federal Communications Commission

In addition to all these, there is an expanding universe of religious or spiritual television networks on pay TV, along with the many family and educational programs that traditional broadcasters offer. While there are still plenty of lewd shows on MTV and F/X, the number of wholesome programs available is also increasing. Parents can just block the channels or shows they find objectionable and steer their kids toward the good stuff—however they define it.

Despite the growth of parental empowerment tools and the cornucopia of family fare now available, many policymakers are still eager to curb the excesses of pay TV and steer the eyes and ears of kids *and parents* by means of regulation. Since direct content regulation is unlikely to pass constitutional muster, lawmakers are now proposing indirect forms of control, including a requirement that cable companies offer packages of "family-friendly" channels. To avoid legislation, most companies have voluntarily offered such packages.[26] Yet few families have expressed interest in subscribing to them, since they lack channels that Mom and Dad might want. Kids aren't the ones paying the monthly cable bill!

"À la carte" regulation is lawmakers' latest effort to reach TV content indirectly. The theory is simple: if we could just mandate that pay TV operators "unbundle" their current program packages and let subscribers choose only the channels they want, then parents could limit their households to wholesome channels. Unfortunately, à la carte isn't that simple in practice, and it almost certainly wouldn't work.

To see why, consider how we have gained access to a 500-channel universe of diverse viewing options on cable and satellite. Those channels didn't appear by magic; companies and investors took risks developing networks to suit diverse interests. Thirty years ago, few could have imagined a world of twenty-four-hour channels devoted to cooking, home renovation, travel, weather, religion, women's issues, and golf. Yet today we have the Food Channel, Home & Garden TV, the Travel

Channel, the Weather Channel, Eternal Word Television Network, Oxygen, the Golf Channel, and countless other niche networks devoted to almost every conceivable human interest. How did this happen?

The answer lies in the very practice of "bundling" that some lawmakers now want to outlaw. Many niche-oriented cable networks exist only because they are bundled with stronger networks. On their own, they would not have survived; indeed, it's doubtful that anyone would have risked launching them in the first place. The business of running a television network is a very different thing from, say, starting up a website. There are enormous fixed costs: scripts, sets, cameras, hosts, actors, props, effects, marketing, and all the supporting staff. Bundling helps firms cover these costs—the big-draw stations in effect subsidize the niche channels—while also satisfying the wide variety of audience tastes.

The anti-bundlers' static view takes the 500-channel universe for granted (just as net-neutrality advocates take the Web's infrastructure for granted); they assume that it will always be with us and that it's just a question of dividing up the pie in different ways. If à la carte were mandated, however, smaller, niche-oriented cable networks would struggle to attract enough subscriber and advertiser support to prosper—or survive.

That's why proponents of à la carte are wrong when they suggest that it would clean up pay TV and allow us to purchase just the "good stuff." Much of the "good stuff" is unlikely to survive in a world of mandatory à la carte regulation. Most family-focused or children's networks, female-oriented channels, and religious programmers oppose à la carte mandates for exactly this reason. They understand that their programs attract only a small subset of the overall universe of viewers. If their networks were not bundled with other channels, they might disappear entirely. Colby May, director of the Faith and Family Broadcasting Coalition, which represents religious broadcasters, last year called à la carte regulation "a dagger aimed at the heart of religious broadcasting in America," a policy that would "decimate religious broadcasting and the wholesome, family-oriented programming carried on niche cable channels."[27]

Meanwhile, the raunchier channels that the culture cops really want to drive off basic cable—MTV, F/X, Comedy Central, Spike, and so on—would probably do just fine in an à la carte universe. They are all among the top twenty networks on cable and satellite TV today, and their shows have a strong following on DVD and on the Internet. Viewers would keep tuning in.

If Congress mandated à la carte, moreover, it would require the forced abrogation of existing contracts between content providers and distributors. That could mean years of litigation and an upending of one of the few business models that have proven successful for traditional media operators in recent years. With competition intensifying and widespread piracy eroding traditional copyright protections, one wonders why lawmakers would want to make it more difficult to produce high-quality, niche-oriented video programming.

Finally, by what right does anyone in government decide how cable or satellite television services—which remain a luxury item, not a birthright—are priced or packaged? If citizens were complaining about the laces bundled with shoes or the tires bundled with cars, would that justify government action?

Just because a certain number of consumers don't like a particular business model doesn't mean the government has license to upend an industry's business arrangements—whether in tires or pay TV—and substitute a grand policy scheme in the name of "consumer choice."

Social networking sites like MySpace and Facebook have enabled millions of Americans—including many teenagers —to create online profiles for communicating with friends or making new ones. But the very openness that drives these platforms' incredible popularity has provoked much worry about underage access to objectionable material and, worse, fears about child predators lurking in cyberspace.

Federal lawmakers have responded with the "Deleting Online Predators Act," which proposed an outright ban on social networking websites in all publicly funded schools and libraries. The measure passed the House of Representatives in 2005 by a lopsided 410–15 vote but didn't clear the Senate the following year.[28] Many state attorneys general have gone further still, calling for mandatory age verification for all visitors to social networking sites.[29] More recently, a Kentucky legislator introduced a truly far-reaching bill that would make it a crime to publish anything anonymously online.[30]

These intrusive regulatory responses are a wild overreaction. They would effectively shut down sites that, generally speaking, are *not* dangerous environments for children and, in fact, have proven wonderful outlets for creativity and community. While it's true that some bad apples have made problems on social networking sites, they tend not to be the predators feared by parents and policymakers.

Abductions by strangers "represent an extremely small portion of all missing children [cases]," noted a 2002 study by the Department of Justice's Office of Juvenile Justice and Delinquency Prevention.[31] The survey found that the vast majority of kidnapping victims were abducted by family, friends of the family, or people who had close relationships with (or the trust of) the minors. Only 115 of the estimated 260,000 abductions—less than 0.1 percent—fit the scenario that parents most fear: complete strangers snatching kids and transporting them miles away.[32] Internet-facilitated abductions by strangers are rarer still.

Further, Internet abductions almost invariably involve a small population of "at-risk" youngsters. A 2004 study from the University of New Hampshire's Crimes Against Children Research Center surveyed more than 2,500 cases in which juveniles became sex-crime victims of people whom they met through the Internet.[33] Only 5 percent of the adult offenders, it turned out, tried to pass themselves off as minors, and only 21 percent lied about their sexual desires. Yet the great majority of victims (83 percent) who met offenders face-to-face went somewhere with them afterward voluntarily—a hotel, movie, or restaurant, for example; many (41 percent) spent at least one night with them; and most (73 percent) willingly met with them more than once.

The researchers also found that most of the youngsters didn't have good relationships with their parents, often reporting a high degree of family conflict or very little parental interaction and mentoring. In some cases, parents were absent from the home altogether. Loneliness and depression were also prevalent in many of the kids. And some of the boys who became willing victims were "gay or questioning" about their sexuality and scared to talk to their parents or educators about it.

In other words, these were at-risk children who needed help, love, understanding, and proper mentoring. It's not surprising that when they didn't get these things, they looked elsewhere for acceptance. "All humans crave companionship and acceptance," observes Nancy E. Willard, author of *Cyber-Safe Kids, Cyber-Savvy Teens*. "Children who, for whatever reason, do not have healthy relationships and do not feel accepted in the 'real world' will be inclined to seek out online connections and communities in which they feel accepted. And this can lead to greater danger online."[34] But it would be mistaken—indeed, absurd—to assume that *all* youth share such problems or would voluntarily meet with older men, let alone engage in sexual activity with them.

Many social networking skeptics bring up a statistic culled from the second Youth Internet Safety Survey, conducted by the National Center for Missing and Exploited Children, which found in 2006 that one out of every seven children has received an online sexual solicitation.[35] That's down from the one-in-five finding from the first survey, released in 2001, but it's still disturbing.

The survey explained, however, that a significant percentage of those "solicitations" were from other kids: when seventeen-year-old Johnny propositions sixteen-year-old Jenny, in other words, it's a solicitation. Teens were delivering such solicitations to one another long before the Internet came along, of course, but parents had no way to track them unless they found a note in a schoolbag or pants pocket. We need to understand that this problem has always been with us—it's just more visible now, since we're measuring things that were previously unmeasurable. It won't disappear with the regulation of the Internet or the imposition of intrusive mandates for age or identity verification on social networking sites.

The effort to impose such mandates is gaining steam, however. Many state attorneys general are demanding that social networking websites verify every user's age or identity, either to keep older people away from youngsters or to keep those youngsters away from social networking sites altogether.[36] But even if such verification were possible—and it probably isn't—it would create a false sense of security for parents and kids, endanger freedom of speech and privacy, and encourage children to abandon generally responsible websites in favor of maverick sites.[37]

Consider how difficult it would be for websites to verify users' ages. Adults can easily create false identities, using publicly accessible records and forging documents. Children would have an even easier time, since they can't be expected to furnish work records, driver's licenses, or credit cards. (They do have birth certificates, Social Security numbers, and school records, but both parents and government officials have long demanded that access to those records be tightly guarded.) Requiring kids to use their parents' credit cards to sign up for social networking sites wouldn't work: credit-card companies make it explicitly clear in their contracts that they don't want their cards used as age-verification proxies. Moreover, credit cards are used for financial transactions, but social networking services are currently free, and the providers won't want to start charging a fee, even a nominal one, that might frighten users away.

The nature of the Internet creates its own problems for age verification. Finding a dependable proof of identity and then reliably matching it to someone thousands of miles away (in another jurisdiction, perhaps, or even another country) is a daunting challenge. In the real world, we perform authentication in person, with a photo or physical description. But the absence of physical contact in social networking renders such methods void. This is why asking parents to vouch for their children's ages would be useless: because websites are far away from the parents, how can the site operator ensure that the person vouching for the child's age is really the parent—or even an adult?

Even if some way existed to make online age verification work, it wouldn't be equivalent to a full-blown background check. Age verification, on its own, doesn't tell us whether or not a person is a convicted sex offender; thus there is a danger of creating a false sense of security by mandating a solution that doesn't address the real problem. It would be unfortunate if parents were led to believe that, once a site had (supposedly) age-verified users, they could drop their guard and let the kids wander freely online.

And even if the original mandate were limited to the most popular social networking sites, children would quickly go elsewhere, necessitating a constant expansion of the permission-based approach. The danger here is that we might encourage more and more kids to "go underground" in an attempt to seek out less regulated sites. It is vitally important that lawmakers do nothing that could force mainstream, domestic social networking sites offshore or, even worse, that could drive the users we are trying to protect to offshore sites. Whatever their concerns about the domestic sites currently available, parents and policymakers should understand that those alternatives are generally more accountable and visible than offshore ones over which we have virtually no influence.

Isn't there a better way to help keep kids safe online, one that wouldn't entangle the Internet in thickets of innovation-strangling new regulation? There is. Call it the "3-E Solution": empowerment, education, and enforcement.[38]

Online-safety education for kids—from parents, educators, and others—is perhaps the most important part of this solution. "You need to take a holistic approach," says Ron Teixeira, executive director of the National Cyber Security Center.[39] Teixeira argues that we should drill basic Internet lessons into our children—the digital equivalent of "don't take candy from strangers"—to ensure that they're prepared for social networking sites and whatever new platforms may follow.[40] "Education is the way you teach children to be proactive, and that will stay with them forever," he concludes.[41] It's about teaching our kids to "use the filter between their ears" and "make responsible decisions about their use of technology," agrees Parry Aftab of Wired Safety.[42] Governments can also help by crafting and promoting sensible online-safety programs.

Parental empowerment is also essential, and luckily parents have numerous tools to monitor and control their children's online experiences. Internet filters can help block objectionable content, as we've seen, but many types of filtering software also now include powerful monitoring tools that let Mom and Dad see each website their kids visit, read every e-mail or instant message they send and receive, and even record every word they type into their word processors.[43] Many tools let parents impose time constraints on their children's computer and Internet use. Some can send parents a periodic report summarizing their children's Internet use and communications, or even show parents screen shots of sites their kids have visited. Some social networking sites are offering their own empowerment tools to parents. In a major 2008 agreement with forty-nine state attorneys general, MySpace has pledged to develop software that will allow parents to keep closer tabs on their kids' online interactions, including seeing the name, age, and location that children are listing on their MySpace accounts.[44]

Parents of preteens who want to let their kids test the social networking waters, but not on the more open sites like MySpace or Facebook, have new options. Smaller social networking sites, such as ZoeysRoom, Imbee, and ClubPenguin, have extremely strict enlistment policies, primarily because they target or allow younger users. Such sites typically filter content for inappropriate material, use live adult monitors to ensure that kids behave themselves, and allow parents to limit conversations or interactions to preapproved friends.

Finally, greater enforcement efforts are necessary to fight online bad guys when they do show up. This doesn't necessarily mean more laws, just better enforcement of existing child-protection statutes. Specifically, Congress needs to make sure that law enforcement officials have the resources they need to protect children from online threats. Higher-quality training and digital forensics are a key part of this. If policymakers feel the urge to pass more legislation, they should start with much stiffer sentences for child abusers. Shockingly, a 2003 Department of Justice study reported that the average sentence for child molesters was approximately seven years and that on average they got out after serving just three years.[45] In 2006, President Bush signed the Adam Walsh Child Protection and Safety Act, which increases mandatory minimum sentences for various crimes against children.[46] That's certainly a helpful step in the right direction, but more can be done.

Where might neophobic policymakers turn their attention next? Perhaps to the still-developing convergence of Internet technologies and traditional media platforms—radio stations on the Web, for example, and T V on cell phones. It wouldn't be surprising if policymakers responded with regulatory convergence, seeking to impose scarcity-era, "public interest" regulations and mandates on the Internet.

For example, in 2007, Senator Mark Pryor of Arizona (a Democrat) introduced the Child Safe Viewing Act, a bill that straddles the divide between the analogue and digital eras.[47] The measure, which passed out of the Senate Commerce Committee after being modified slightly, requires that the FCC study "advanced blocking technologies" for parents that can operate independently of existing rating systems. Additional *private* parental controls and rating systems are always welcome, of course; and a plethora of them already exist. But more FCC study of independent controls might undermine existing tools and rating systems. Pryor's bill also stipulates that the FCC must examine the effectiveness of parental controls across a wide variety of distribution systems, including "wired, wireless, and Internet platforms." This would enable the FCC to expand its content-control efforts.

Another example of a well-meaning measure that could open a Pandora's box of unintended consequences is the Cyber Safety for Kids Act, sponsored by Senator Pryor and his Democratic colleague from Montana, Max Baucus. The bill proposes mandatory website labeling for material that is "harmful to minors." The National Telecommunications and Information Administration (NTIA) would be required to develop tags for such content—essentially, a government rating system for websites. These tags would then need to be registered with ICANN, the international organization that coordinates domain-name policy, though it is unclear what would happen if other countries refused to employ the same system. Finally, the measure requires that age-verification mechanisms be used to block access to such material once the tags are in place. The proposal seems both unworkable and unconstitutional. Some groups would be sympathetic to the idea of tagging sites deemed bad for children, no doubt. But how would "harmful to minors" be defined? What else might lawmakers want to "tag" for other purposes? Calling the law a slippery slope would be an understatement.

Any way you cut it, the media cornucopia runs the risk of being subjected to a massive Nanny State intrusion on content grounds in coming years. But just because something is novel doesn't mean that it's dangerous or that new government regulations are necessary to protect us from it.

CHAPTER FIVE

CAMPAIGN-FINANCE REFORM'S
WAR ON POLITICAL SPEECH

ONE OF THE biggest dangers to media freedom—and political speech in general—comes not from new media regulations but from campaign-finance rules, especially those spawned by the 2002 Bipartisan Campaign Reform Act, known as McCain-Feingold. While cosponsored by the Republican "maverick" senator and now presidential candidate John McCain (along with Russ Feingold), the bill passed only because of overwhelming Democratic support. It's easy to see why liberals have spearheaded the nation's experiment with campaign-finance regulation. In the name of getting "big-money corruption" out of politics, election-law reforms obstruct the kinds of political speech—campaign ads and possibly even the feisty editorializing of the new media—that escape the filter of the mainstream press, the academy, and Hollywood; and these left-wing fiefdoms remain free from regulation. Campaign-finance reform, by steadily expanding "government's control of the political campaigns that decide who controls government," advances "liberalism's program of extending government supervision of life," remarks the columnist George Will.[1]

The irony of campaign-finance reform is that the "corruption" it targets seems to be quite limited in reality. Studies galore have found that campaign contributions have little or no influence on legislators' votes. Ideological commitment, party positions, and constituents' wishes are what motivate the typical politician's actions in office. Of course, some will retort, the corruption is hidden; its effects lie in what Congress *doesn't* do—like enacting big new environmental taxes. But as Will notes, "[T]hat charge is impossible to refute by disproving a negative." Even so, such suspicions are transforming election law into what the journalist Jonathan Rauch calls "an engine of unlimited political regulation."[2]

McCain-Feingold, the latest and scariest step in that direction, made it a felony for corporations, nonprofit advocacy groups, and labor unions to run ads that criticize—or even name or show—members of Congress within sixty days of a federal election, when such quintessentially political speech might actually persuade voters. It also forbade political parties from soliciting or spending "soft money" contributions to publicize the principles and ideas they stand for. Amending the already baffling campaign-finance rules from the 1970s and before, McCain-Feingold's long list of restrictions and its onerous reporting requirements on funding sources—filling a dense 300-page book—have made it unwise and potentially ruinous to run for office, contribute to a candidate, or advocate for a cause without an attorney at hand. Not for nothing has Justice Clarence Thomas denounced McCain-Feingold's "unprecedented restrictions" as an "assault on the free exchange of ideas."[3]

Campaign-finance reform has a squeaky-clean image, but the truth is that this speech-throttling legislation has been tainted with dubious motives from its very origin. Bradley Smith, a law professor and former chairman of the Federal Election Commission, points out that the first federal campaign-finance law, the 1907 Tillman Act, which banned corporate contributions to federal campaigns, was sponsored by Senator Ben Tillman, a South Carolina Democrat and a notorious racist who encouraged the lynching of black voters and helped create Jim Crow in the South. "The new law fit neatly with his segregationist agenda," explains Smith, "since corporate 'money power' primarily backed anti-segregationist Republican politicians."[4]

McCain-Feingold was partly the result of a hoax perpetrated by a handful of liberal foundations, led by the venerable Pew Charitable Trusts. Ryan Sager, a reporter, exposed the scam when he got hold of a 2004 videotape of a former Pew official, Sean Treglia, telling a roomful of journalists and professors how Pew and other foundations spent years bankrolling various experts, ostensibly independent nonprofits (including Democracy 21 and the Center for Public Integrity), and media outlets (NPR got $1.2 million for "news coverage of financial influence in political decision-making")—all aimed at fooling Washington into thinking that Americans were clamoring for reform, when in truth there was little public pressure to clean up the system. "The target group for all this activity was 535 people in Washington," said Treglia matter-of-factly, referring to Congress. "The idea was to create an impression that a mass movement was afoot—that everywhere they looked, in academic institutions, in the business community, in religious groups, in ethnic groups, everywhere, people were talking about reform."

Treglia urged grantees to keep Pew's role hush-hush. "If Congress thought this was a Pew effort," he confided, "it'd be worthless. It'd be 20 million bucks thrown down the drain." At one point, late in the congressional debate over McCain-Feingold, "we had a scare," Treglia said. "George Will stumbled across a report we had done. . . . He started to reference the fact that Pew was playing a large role . . . [and] that it was a liberal attempt to hoodwink Congress. . . . The good news, from my perspective, was that journalists . . . just didn't care and nobody followed up." The hoaxers—eight left-wing foundations, including George Soros's Open Society Institute and the Ford Foundation—spent $123 million between 1994 and early 2005 on trying to get other people's money out of politics, Sager reports. That is nearly 90 percent of the sum spent by the entire campaign-finance lobby over the same period.[5]

The ultimate dream of the reformers is a rigidly egalitarian society, where government makes sure that every individual's influence over politics is exactly the same, regardless of wealth. Scrutinize the pronouncements of campaign-finance reform advocates and you'll see how the meaning of "corruption" morphs into "inequality of influence." The Pew-backed Democracy 21, for instance, works to eliminate "the undue influence of big money in American politics." "It's time to let all our citizens have an equal voice," thundered Rep. John Lewis, a Democrat from Georgia, in the debate over McCain-Feingold.[6] This notion of corruption—really a Marxoid opposition to inequality of wealth—would have horrified the Founding Fathers, who believed in private property with its attendant inequalities, and who trusted in the clash of factions to ensure that none oppressed the others. The Founders would have seen the reformers' utopian schemes, in which the power of government makes all equally weak, as the embodiment of tyranny.[7]

Leading theorists of campaign-finance reform—such as Edward Foley, a law professor at Ohio State University (and former Ohio state solicitor); Richard Hasen, a law professor at Loyola; and Ronald Dworkin, the radical redistributionist philosopher—want to replace privately financed campaigns with a system in which government would guarantee "equal dollars per voter," as Foley puts it, perhaps by giving all Americans the same number of political "coupons," which they could then redeem on the political activities of their choice.[8] The government would then ban all other political expenditures and require all political groups to get operating licenses, with stiff criminal penalties for violators. The experts have even started calling for draconian media restrictions in order to achieve their egalitarian aims. In Foley's view, the chilling of speech is "the necessary price we must pay in order to have an electoral system that guarantees equal opportunity for all." But when these experts pen law-review articles with titles like "Campaign Finance Laws and the Rupert Murdoch Problem," you know it isn't the *New York Times* or CBS News that they have in mind.

This isn't just ivory-tower speculation; the push to eliminate privately financed campaigns has some heavyweight politicians behind it. "Reform is a process," said McCain in 2003. "It is not a one-time fight."[9] True to his word, McCain and several cosponsors followed up the Bipartisan Campaign Reform Act with the "Our Democracy, Our Airwaves Act of 2003," or

McCain-Feingold II, as some called it. Though it didn't pass, McCain-Feingold II would have required broadcasters to run twelve hours of "candidate-centered and issue-centered programming" in the six weeks prior to primary and general elections—without giving them any control over those twelve hours (half of which would have had to run during prime time). It would also have created a voucher system for the purchase of airtime for political advertisements, financed by an annual spectrum-use fee on all broadcast license holders.[10] In sum, the legislation would have forced broadcast stations to pay a tax to the federal government that would, in turn, finance a pool of funds that politicians could turn around and spend to run ads on those very stations! The measure took a big step toward the Foley-Hasen-Dworkin dream of incorruptible politics—which would be a politics without freedom.

Recently, campaign-finance reformers put the blogosphere in their crosshairs. When the Federal Election Commission wrote specific rules in 2002 to implement McCain-Feingold, it voted 4–2 to exempt the Web. After all, observed the majority of three Republicans and one Democrat (the agency divides its seats evenly between the two parties), Congress didn't list the Internet among the "public communications"—everything from television to roadside billboards—that the FEC should regulate. Further, "the Internet is virtually a limitless resource, where the speech of one person does not interfere with the speech of anyone else," reasoned Republican commissioner Michael Toner. "Whereas campaign finance regulation is meant to ensure that money in politics does not corrupt candidates or officeholders, or create the appearance thereof, such rationales cannot plausibly be applied to the Internet, where on-line activists can communicate about politics with millions of people at little or no cost."[11]

But the chief House architects of campaign-finance reform—joined by Senators McCain and Feingold—sued, claiming that the Internet was one big "loophole" that allowed big money to keep on corrupting our political system. A federal judge agreed and ordered the FEC to look into clamping down on Web politics. Commissioner Smith and the two other Republicans on the FEC couldn't persuade their Democratic colleagues to appeal the ruling.

The FEC thus plunged into what Smith called a "bizarre" rulemaking process that could have shackled the political blogosphere. This would be a particular disaster for the right, which has maintained a competitive position with the left in the blogosphere, despite the emergence of big liberal sites like Daily Kos. Reaching a growing and influential audience—hundreds of thousands of readers weekly (including most journalists) for the top conservative sites—the blogosphere has enabled the right to counter the biases of the liberal media mainstream. Without the blogosphere, Howell Raines would still be the editor of the *New York Times*; Dan Rather would only now be retiring, garlanded with praise; and John Kerry might be president of the United States, assuming that CBS News had gotten away with the falsehood about President Bush's military service that the diligent bloggers at PowerLine, Little Green Footballs, and other sites swiftly debunked.

Should the hundreds of political blogs that have sprouted over the last few years—today's version of the Revolutionary era's political pamphlets—be classified as "press" and thus be exempt from FEC regulations? Liberal reform groups like Democracy 21 say no. "We do not believe anyone described as a 'blogger' is by definition entitled to the benefit of the press exemption," they collectively opined in a brief to the FEC. "While some bloggers may provide a function very similar to more classical media activities, and thus could reasonably be said to fall within the exemption, others surely do not." The key test, the groups claimed, should be whether the blogger is performing a "legitimate press function."[12] But who decides what is a legitimate press function? And what clause in the Constitution grants the authority to make that judgment?

A first draft of proposed FEC Web rules, leaked to the RedState blog in March 2006, would have regulated all but tiny, password-protected political sites, so bloggers had cause to be worried. Without a general exemption, political blogs could easily find themselves in regulatory hell. Say it's a presidential race, Barack Obama versus John McCain. You run a wildly opinionated and popular group blog—call it No to Obama—that rails daily about the perils of an Obama presidency and sometimes republishes McCain campaign material. Is your blog making "contributions" to McCain? Maybe. The FEC, after all, says that a "contribution" includes "any gift, subscription, loan, advance, or deposit of money or *anything of value* made by any person for the purpose of influencing any election for Federal office" (our italics). If your anti-Obama blog spends more than $1,000, you could also find it reclassified as a "political committee." Then you've got countless legal requirements and funding limits to worry about.

In such a regulated Web-world, bloggers and operators of

political sites would have to get press exemptions on a case-by-case basis. The results, as the election-law expert Bob Bauer explains, would be "unpredictable, highly sensitive to subtle differences in facts and to the political environment of the moment." Even when the outcome is happy, "a favorable result is still an act of noblesse oblige by a government well aware that if it turns down a request, the disappointed applicant is left with litigation as the only option."[13]

Websites would live in fear of Kafkaesque FEC enforcement actions, often triggered by complaints from political rivals. "If the matter is based on a complaint," notes Allison Hayward, a former FEC counsel, "the 'respondent' will receive a letter from the FEC with the complaint and will be asked to show why the FEC shouldn't investigate." An investigation involves "the usual tools of civil litigation-document requests, depositions, briefs, and the like." The outcome can take months "or longer" to determine, says Hayward. "If a complaint is filed against you, there will be a flurry of activity while you respond, then perhaps silence—then another letter will arrive and you will be required to respond promptly, then maybe nothing again for months." Most political bloggers aren't paid reporters or commentators; they're just ordinary citizens with day jobs who like to exercise their right to voice their opinions. If doing so without a lawyer puts them or their families at risk, many would simply stop blogging about politics—or never start.

If you think such fretting is silly, says Bradley Smith, consider the case of Bill Liles, who faced an FEC inquiry when Smith was commissioner. In 2000, a businessman named Harvey Bass in the little Texas town of Muleshoe painted SAVE OUR NATION: VOTE DEMOCRAT AL GORE FOR

PRESIDENT on a beat-up box and plunked it on his furniture store's porch. Sick of looking at the sign, Liles and a friend pasted a "bigger and better" poster praising George W. Bush on a trailer and parked it right across from Bass's store. This was too much for another local, Don Dyer, who complained to the FEC that Liles's sign lacked the mandated disclosures about who paid for it and whether Bush had signed off on it.

Though the FEC in the end let Liles and his fellow activists off the hook, the men may have broken not just disclosure rules but any number of other regulations, recalls Smith. If they had spent more than $250 on their sign, for example, they would have failed to report the expenditure to the FEC, as required. "Total statutory penalties could have easily exceeded $25,000," Smith observes.[14]

Another example: Kirk Shelmerdine, a NASCAR driver, stuck a BUSH–CHENEY '04 decal on his car's advertising space. The FEC blasted him for making an unreported campaign donation. Or consider the effort of a conservative group, Citizens United, to release a film in 2004 responding to Michael Moore's anti-Bush *Fahrenheit 9/11*. The FEC told the group to forget about advertising its film—or broadcasting it publicly—close to the election, lest McCain-Feingold restrictions apply. A similar judgment fell upon a pro-Bush, pro-gun-rights movie by David Hardy, a Second Amendment activist. By contrast, Moore's movie got an FEC pass because he, unlike the conservative producers, was in the (unregulated) movie business.[15]

How different is the activism of Liles or Shelmerdine or Citizens United from that of many political bloggers? The media differ, but all are simply voicing their opinions. In the end, the FEC decided to leave Web politics alone for the most part, instead of establishing the extensive oversight it had planned; the fierce outburst from political bloggers on both the right and the left when they discovered their freedom of speech under fire clearly scared the regulators off. But with McCain-Feingold in place, there's no guarantee that the commission won't expand its reach at a later point. "If the history of campaign finance regulation is any guide," says Michael Toner, "once the FEC exercises jurisdiction over the Internet, the Commission's initial set of regulations, even if narrowly tailored, are likely to lead to broader regulation in the future." Right after McCain-Feingold became law, Senator Feingold predicted: "It is only a beginning. It is a modest reform. . . . There will be other reforms." Most campaign-finance reformers share that regulate-to-the-max outlook, aiming—swiftly or incrementally—to close all the "loopholes."

Imagine the regulatory apparatus needed to enforce such a regime in a world of proliferating media and abundant speech. Restrictions might have worked in an age of scarcity, when a finite number of platforms existed and the biggest were easily identifiable. But how many FEC bureaucrats would be needed to monitor every renegade political blogger? Or would the government deputize ISPs to monitor Internet traffic in an attempt to weed out those bytes tagged as "illegal electioneering"? More insidiously, perhaps lawmakers, recognizing the enforcement challenge at hand, would pay snitches to inform on fellow bloggers who run afoul of the law.

Even if the FEC limited its focus to policing online political advertising, is there really a chance that any individual, political party, or special-interest group could ever buy up all the ad time on the Web? Of course not—they couldn't even buy up 0.1 percent of it. But without tight restrictions on Web communications, won't some of those groups unduly influence the election process by paying bloggers or other website operators to write favorable things about a specific candidate or issue, hoodwinking the public? Maybe, but in our increasingly crowded blogosphere with its cacophony of voices, no one website or blog rules in the way that a broadcaster might have dominated a community in the past. Even if some especially popular blogs were taking political money to drum up support for a given candidate, moreover, it's likely that others would catch on and start asking questions, or even do some detective work and figure out who was really behind the effort. Considering what bloggers did to Dan Rather and CBS News, how long would it take a pack of them to get to the bottom of such a racket?[16]

Minimal disclosure requirements could be used to let the public know who is funding a specific outlet. But it would be better to place any such requirements on the people who give the money instead of the websites that receive it. Those who write the big checks already file reports at the FEC, so they can disclose that information as part of their typical filing process. It would be a mistake to place onerous FEC filing burdens and disclosure mandates on bloggers or other website operators simply because somebody might have tossed a few bucks into their tip jars.

Realizing that McCain-Feingold is out of control, a liberty-minded Texas Republican, Jeb Hensarling, introduced the Online Freedom of Speech Act in the House in April 2005. (Harry Reid has sponsored identical legislation in the Senate, showing that not all Democrats are lost on the issue.) This bill would have reinforced the Internet's current regulation-free status by excluding blogs and various other Web communications from campaign-finance strictures. Brought to an expedited vote in early November under special rules that required a two-thirds majority, the bill—opposed strenuously by the campaign-finance reform movement—failed. "Today's action marks a sad day for one of our nation's most sacred rights: freedom of speech," reflected Speaker Dennis Hastert. "The last thing this Congress should be doing is trying to stifle public debate online."

The House Democrats torpedoed the Online Freedom of Speech Act, but they had surprising help from about three dozen Republicans. Why did so many normally staunch opponents of restrictions on campaign speech decide to shift camp? One possible explanation, perhaps cynical: it's hard to unseat incumbents, given their advantages of name recognition, free media exposure, and an easier time raising donations. Campaign-finance rules make it even harder for their rivals to get attention. Notably, after Congress began campaign-finance restrictions in the 1970s, reelection rates for incumbents began to rise. Once in office, some Republicans may suddenly like McCain-Feingold's power to shield them from criticism, just as some may develop a sudden keenness for media "fairness" mandates.

* * *

95

It's not just the blogosphere or the occasional conservative movie in an election season that's at risk. The left has also tried to use campaign-finance reform—not McCain-Feingold but equally onerous state regulations—in its ongoing efforts to shush political talk radio. Consider what happened recently in Washington State as a warning.

Early in 2005, the Democrat-controlled legislature passed, and Governor Christine Gregoire (also a Democrat) signed, a bill boosting the state's gasoline tax by a whopping 9.5 cents per gallon over the next four years, supposedly to fund transportation projects. Thinking that their taxes were already plenty high and that the state's corrupt Transportation Department would just squander the gas-tax revenues, some citizens organized an initiative campaign to junk the new levy, calling their effort No New Gas Tax.

Two popular conservative talk radio hosts, Kirby Wilbur and John Carlson, explained why the gas tax was bad news and urged listeners to supply the 225,000 petition signatures needed to get the rollback initiative on the November ballot, though they played no official role in the campaign and regularly featured defenders as well as opponents of the tax hike on their programs. With the hosts' help, the petition drive got almost twice the number of needed signatures; but the ballot initiative—strongly opposed by labor unions, the state's liberal media, environmental groups, and other powerful interests—narrowly lost.

Meantime, a group of pro-tax politicians sued No New Gas Tax, arguing that Wilbur's and Carlson's on-air commentaries were "in-kind contributions" and that the antitax campaign had failed to report them to the proper state authorities. The suit sought to stop NNGT from accepting any more of these "contributions" until it disclosed their worth—though how the initiative's organizers could control media discussions or calculate their monetary value remained unclear. The complaint also socked NNGT with civil penalties, attorneys' fees and costs, and other damages. Even more offensively, to litigate the suit, the politicians hired a private law firm, Foster Pepper & Shefelman, that served as bond counsel to Washington State and could thus clean up from the state's plan to sell bonds backed by the gas tax. Appearance of corruption, anyone?

The real targets of the suit were clearly Wilbur and Carlson or, more accurately, their corporate employer, Fisher Communications. If NNGT *received* the "contributions," that meant Fisher had *sent* them by broadcasting Wilbur's and Carlson's support for the initiative. Washington law limits contributions in the final three weeks of a political campaign to $5,000. Depending on how one measured the dollar worth of on-air "contributions," Fisher could thus face big fines and criminal penalties if it let Wilbur and Carlson keep talking about the gas tax. "Thankfully, Fisher assured us that we *could* keep talking about the subject on the air, and we did," Wilbur says.[17] The judge ruled in favor of the pro-tax politicians, though he finessed the $5,000 limit by ruling only on the "contributions" that occurred prior to the campaign's final three weeks.

The Institute for Justice, a libertarian legal defense group, then entered the fray, filing both an appeal to the Washington State Supreme Court and a counterclaim against the politicians behind the suit. "I think this case presented a substantial issue under the First Amendment," explained Bill Maurer, an attorney with the institute. "This [was] one of the most important cases nationally about the right of the press to speak freely, without the interference of the government or regulation of the government—because the power to regulate is the power to suppress."[18] Had the appeal lost, the days of political talk radio could have been over not only in Washington State but everywhere. "McCain-Feingold could definitely be used in the same fashion," Maurer says. In fact, the prosecutors in the case said that McCain-Feingold permitted them to do this. "But pretty much any state that has campaign-finance laws that restrict contributions is subject to this abuse, too," adds Maurer.

Thankfully, the Washington State Supreme Court reversed the decision in April 2007, but as Smith points out, "the court didn't base its decision on the First Amendment, instead ruling that the statute in question didn't cover radio talk. In a footnote, the court specifically noted that 'nothing in our decision today forecloses the legislature, or the people via the initiative process, from limiting the statutory media exemption.'"[19]

All this points to an enormous question: Why should any American need government permission to express himself? Instead of a media exemption, the blogger Glenn Reynolds sarcastically comments, maybe we need a "free speech exception, in which you are allowed to say what you want about political candidates without fear of prosecution by the government."[20]

You'd think that the Supreme Court of the United States would have rescued the new media—and the nation—from all this regulatory tyranny. President Bush reportedly agreed not to veto McCain-Feingold only because he was sure the Court would do it for him and he could thereby avoid riling John

McCain. After all, the language of the First Amendment, to quote it again, is unambiguous: "Congress shall make no law . . . abridging the freedom of speech, or of the press." The Supreme Court in recent years has extended First Amendment protection to nude dancing, animated online kiddy porn, flag burning, tobacco advertising, and cross burning. For its original architects, of course, the First Amendment's chief aim was to protect *political* speech, including the right to criticize the government. The notion that government could restrict the political speech of some—which is what campaign-finance rules do—would have been the very definition of tyranny for men like Samuel Adams or James Madison. How could the justices not want to stop the juggernaut of campaign-finance regulation?

Yet the Supreme Court's 5–4 ruling in *McConnell v. FEC* approved almost all of McCain-Feingold. The 2003 decision shocked many—it means we now live in a country that affords more constitutional protections to Internet pornography than to political speech leading up to elections; but the Court's "evolving" jurisprudence in the area of campaign finance should have made it not all that surprising. For the past three decades, the Court has steadily chopped away at constitutional protection for political speech when campaign finance is at issue. In its 1976 *Buckley v. Valeo* decision, the Court struck the first blow by authorizing the "balancing" of free-speech concerns with the "governmental interest" in preventing "the actuality and the appearance of corruption."

The idea of "balance" has become a campaign-reform commonplace, expressed bluntly a few years ago by the former House minority leader Richard Gephardt (a Democrat): "What we have is two important values in direct conflict: freedom of speech and our desire for healthy campaigns in a healthy democracy." But as the commentator Thomas Sowell retorted, whatever Gephardt's definition of a healthy campaign is, "it is not part of the Constitution of the United States—and free speech is."[21] Free speech, in fact, is the bedrock of our healthy democracy. For McCain, though, it appears to be secondary. "I would rather have a clean government than one where, quote, First Amendment rights are being respected, that has become corrupt," he told the radio host Don Imus.[22]

Buckley's loose language is troubling, too. "The 'appearance of corruption' can mean anything," says Bradley Smith. "If the 'appearance of corruption' is sufficient to justify regulation, the practical effect is to eliminate the need for the government to show any justification for the regulation in question."[23] In fact, even John McCain, now incorruptible after his involvement in the Keating Five scandal, might appear corrupt. Several aides from his 2000 presidential run, including his former campaign manager, press secretary, finance director, and legal counsel, wound up working for the Reform Institute, a nonprofit group dedicated to (you guessed it) campaign-finance reform—though it seemed to be primarily a nascent McCain for President 2008 campaign. Back in 2005, the Associated Press discovered, when Cablevision sought approval for a pricing change from the Senate Commerce Committee, then chaired by McCain, the company developed a sudden interest in campaign-finance reform and gave the Reform Institute a $200,000 "soft" donation. Looks fishy, no?[24]

Making matters worse, the Supreme Court's 1990 *Austin v. Michigan Chamber of Commerce* decision redefined "corruption" to mean not just the exchange of political favors for money—seemingly *Buckley*'s view, though the Court's opinion is vague—but also "the corrosive and distorting effects of immense aggregations of wealth that are accumulated with the help of the corporate form and that have little or no correlation to the public's support for the corporation's political ideas." In other words, the Court's majority fully embraced the Inequality = Corruption thinking of the campaign-finance reformers. If corporations had or appeared to have too much influence, government could now stamp out this "corruption" by shutting them up, as McCain-Feingold has done, rather than by the checks and balances of faction against faction, as the Founders envisioned.

In his powerful *McConnell* dissent, Justice Thomas spelled out "the chilling endpoint" of the Court's reasoning: "outright regulation of the press," which is exactly what the campaign-reform theorists ultimately seek. "Media companies can run pro-candidate editorials as easily as nonmedia corporations can pay for advertisements," Thomas explained. "Media corporations are influential. There is little doubt that the editorials and commentary they run can affect elections." The Supreme Court has found little to distinguish media from nonmedia corporations. Asked Thomas: "What is to stop a future Congress from determining that the press is 'too influential,' and that the 'appearance of corruption' is significant when media organizations endorse candidates or run 'slanted' or 'biased' news stories in favor of candidates or parties?" Answer: nothing. "Although today's opinion does not expressly strip the press of First Amendment protection," Thomas warned, "there is no principle of law or logic that would prevent the application of the Court's reasoning in that setting. The press now operates at the whim of Congress."

In 2007, with the First Amendment–friendly John Roberts and Samuel Alito now on the bench, the Supreme Court stepped back "from the abyss," as Smith puts it. In *Randall v. Sorrell*, the Court struck down expenditure limits and extremely low contribution limits in Vermont; and in *Wisconsin Right to Life v. FEC*, the Court argued that McCain-Feingold's limits on broadcast ads mentioning a candidate within two months of an election might have exceptions. But free-speech fans shouldn't get too excited: McCain-Feingold remains the law of the land. Both decisions were by narrow majorities of 5–4, with two members of those majorities over seventy years old. And it's unlikely "that a Democratic president, or a President McCain, would appoint pro-speech judges to the court," says Smith.[25]

The latest campaign-finance controversy involves SpeechNow.org, a group formed by the free-speech activist David Keating, which plans to buy ads calling for citizens to vote for pro-free-speech politicians and against those who hold a more "balanced" view of the First Amendment. The organization, which will disclose all its contributions and expenditures to the FEC, is made up of independent citizens, spending their own money; it refuses corporate and union money, doesn't coordinate its work with any political party, and shells out zilch in donations to politicians or parties. But campaign-finance law and the FEC define SpeechNow.org as a political committee and thus obliged to comply with extremely strict funding limits.

The group has filed suit in the U.S. District Court for the

District of Columbia challenging the constitutionality of requiring groups of independent citizens to register as PACs. An editorial by Bradley Smith and Steve Simpson, an attorney with the Institute for Justice, remarks of this case: "For the first time, federal courts will be asked to decide whether independent political speech by groups of individual American citizens has the full protection of the First Amendment."[26]

Perhaps the liberal media will stop cheering for campaign-finance reform when they realize that their own First Amendment rights are at stake, too.

CONCLUSION

IN HIS REMARKABLE 1994 book *Orwell's Revenge*, Peter Huber predicted the media cornucopia, the sensorium of ideas and imagination, that now surrounds us and underscored a fundamental truth about the technology of communication: "Better communicating machines produce more—not less—communication, more—not less—free expression, more—not less —political involvement, more—not less—freedom of thought."[1]

Many will object to this anarchic abundance, as Huber captures in an imagined confrontation between *1984*'s O'Brien, a monster of control, and Winston Smith, now seen as a prophet of technological liberation. Without censorship and enforced order in the mediasphere, O'Brien charges, a torrent of calumny, "necrophilic reveries," and conspiracy-mongering will be unleashed. The social order will collapse, "the individual's freedom becomes the community's slavery."

Smith, O'Brien's prisoner, sweeps away such concerns. The new media technology "will give us necrophilic reveries," he acknowledges, "but it will also create room for the art of angels. It will supply passion but also reason. It will spread propaganda but also private discourse. It will give us spies but also the distance to elude them. It will carry the proclamations of generals before battle, the speeches of führers and prime ministers, the solidarity songs of public schools and left-wing political parties, national anthems, temperance tracts, papal encyclicals and sermons against gambling and contraception—and it will also carry the chorus of raspberries from all the millions of common men to whom these sentiments make no appeal." Sure, electronic thugs will be empowered, as will the Thought Police. "But in the middle," Smith concludes, "stand the great mass of men, simple, honest, and sane."[2] Such people will make sanity prevail; they make the risk of freedom worth taking. The new media abundance will improve democracy, fire creativity, and expand individual and communal knowledge and know-how.

In fact, it is already doing these things. Yet our O'Briens, as we have shown in this brief polemic, are legion. Most today are on the left—illiberal liberals who believe the risk of freedom not worth taking. Motivated by the naked desire for political control, a reactionary fear of the new, or genuine if misguided views on equality and fairness in the media, they threaten to enact regulations that will strangle or at least cripple this social development before it can begin to reach its potential. Those on the right are not free from these impulses, either. But they, as the prime beneficiaries of media abundance—of all the conservative and libertarian talk shows and websites that would suffer in a media landscape remade by the Democratic Party and liberal activists—should embrace, defend, and expand the freedom that made it possible.

We can sum up the practical imperatives of our book in the following Manifesto for Media Freedom:

Conclusion

- Embrace the dazzling variety of modern media—a cornucopia that gives people the freedom to choose among a rich and growing array of information and entertainment options. Never has it been easier to become an informed democratic citizen.

- Reject any effort to reimpose the Fairness Doctrine, either within Congress or at the FCC. Besides being hostile to free speech and subject to political abuse, it would substantially reduce the variety of voices (especially conservative voices) competing in the modern agora.

- Liberate media operators from archaic restrictions and mandates that limit their flexibility to respond to the radical changes occurring in the media marketplace.

- Say no to new "localism" or "public interest" mandates that would impose yet more regulatory burdens on broadcast television and radio operators already struggling to remain competitive in the new media universe. These mandates should also be dismissed as sly attempts to reinstate Fairness Doctrine-esque content controls over the market.

- Allow broadband Internet providers to manage more actively the data pulsing through their cables, fiber optics, phone lines, and wireless connections, thus creating a twenty-first-century telecommunications infrastructure. Net neutrality is a bad idea—a form of infrastructure socialism that would stifle innovation and threaten a major Web slowdown.

- Don't fear new media!

Conclusion

- Reject "à la carte" mandates on cable and satellite providers that would decimate the vibrant diversity of programming on pay T V today, hitting family-friendly and religious broadcasters particularly hard.

- Block federal, state, or local efforts to regulate video game content or to replace the industry's excellent voluntary rating system with a government-imposed system. Parents have all the tools they need to monitor their children's consumption of video games without an expanded Nanny State's intervention.

- Encourage parental empowerment and education-based strategies to address concerns about children's online safety instead of banning social networking websites or other online content.

- Take steps to roll back the most onerous elements of modern campaign-finance law and to protect new media outlets and forms of political expression from speech-stifling restrictions.

NOTES

CHAPTER ONE: THE MEDIA CORNUCOPIA AND ITS CRITICS

1 Federal Communications Commission, *In the Matter of 2002 Biennial Regulatory Review: Review of the Commission's Broadcast Ownership Rules and Other Rules Adopted Pursuant to Section 202 of the Telecommunications Act of 1996*, FCC 03-127, June 2, 2003, p. 4, http://hraunfoss.fcc.gov/edocs_public/attachmatch/ FCC-03-127A1.pdf.

2 During a committee hearing several months later, in what was apparently supposed to be a humorous gesture, Rep. Markey introduced an amendment that would have deemed the new FCC cross-ownership rules to be "indecent" and require commissioners who supported the rule to watch the movie *Citizen Kane* over and over "until they flinch at the word 'Rosebud.'" Quoted in Terry Lane, "House Commerce Committee Raise 'Indecency' Fines to $500,000," *Communications Daily*, March 4, 2004, p. 2.

3 Quoted in "Lawmakers Predict Revolt over Media Dictatorships," *Broadcasting & Cable*, July 23, 2003, http://www.broadcastingcable.com/ index.asp?layout=articlePrint&articleID=CA313012.

4 Quoted in Terry Lane, "Hinchey Pushes Fairness Doctrine Bill to CWA," *Communications Daily*, March 31, 2004, p. 9.

5 "Dean Vows to 'Break Up Giant Media Enterprises,'" Drudge Report, December 2, 2003, http://www.drudgereport.com/dean1.htm; Bill McConnell, "Dean Threatens to Break Up Media Giants," *Broadcasting & Cable*, December 3, 2003, http://www.broadcastingcable.com/ index.asp?layout=articlePrint&articleID=CA339546. See also Brian C. Anderson, *South Park Conservatives: The Revolt against Liberal Media Bias* (Washington, D.C.: Regnery, 2005), ch. 3, "Fighting Back: Conservative Talk Radio," pp. 33–50.

6 XM and Sirius, annual SEC reports.

7   Federal Communications Commission, various annual reports on competition in video markets.

8   *The Magazine Handbook 2004/05* (New York: Magazine Publishers of America, 2004), p. 5, http://www.magazine.org/content/Files/MPA_handbook_04.pdf; *The Magazine Handbook 2007/08* (New York: Magazine Publishers of America, 2008), p. 5, http://www.magazine.org/content/Files/magHandbook07_08.pdf.

9   See John Podhoretz, "The News Mausoleum," *Commentary*, May 2008, pp. 37–41. "The prospect is a very stark one for people who work in, write, and edit newspapers," notes Podhoretz.

10 "Internet Domain Survey Host Count," Internet Systems Consortium, http://www.isc.org/index.pl?/ops/ds/.

11 "About Us," Technorati, http://www.technorati.com/about/.

12 Quoted on *NewsHour with Jim Lehrer*, April 2001, http://www.pbs.org/newshour/media/conglomeration/auletta.html.

13 Mark Cooper, *Media Ownership and Democracy in the Digital Information Age* (Stanford, Calif.: Center for Internet and Society, Stanford University Law School, 2003), http://cyberlaw.stanford.edu/blogs/cooper/archives/mediabooke.pdf.

14 See Ben Compaine, "Domination Fantasies," *Reason*, January 2004, cover story.

15 David Westin, "Don't Blame the Networks," *Washington Post*, September 30, 2004, p. A19.

16 Herbert Simon, "Designing Organizations for an Information-Rich World," in *Computers, Communications and the Public Interest*, ed. Martin Greenberger (Baltimore: Johns Hopkins Press, 1971), pp. 40–41.

17 Todd Gitlin, *Media Unlimited: How the Torrent of Images and Sounds Overwhelms Our Lives* (New York: Henry Holt & Company, 2002); Barry Schwartz, *The Paradox of Choice: Why More Is Less* (New York: Ecco, 2004).

18 Chris Anderson, *The Long Tail: Why the Future of Business Is Selling Less of More* (New York: Hyperion, 2006).

19 Nicholas Negroponte, *Being Digital* (New York: Knopf, 1995).

20 Cass Sunstein, *Republic.com* (Princeton, N.J.: Princeton University Press, 2001), p. 123.

21 Schwartz, *The Paradox of Choice*, p. 18.

22 Quoted in Paul Farhi, "Voters Are Harder to Reach as Media Outlets Multiply," *Washington Post*, June 16, 2004, http://www.washingtonpost.com/wp-dyn/articles/A44697-2004Jun15.html.

Notes

23 See Marc Gunther, "The Extinction of Mass Culture," CNN-Money.com, http://money.cnn.com/2006/07/11/news/economy/pluggedin_gunther.fortune/index.htm.

24 See Eric Burns's lively history, *Infamous Scribblers: The Founding Fathers and the Rowdy Beginnings of American Journalism* (New York: PublicAffairs, 2006). Jefferson, Franklin, and Hamilton were right in the thick of it.

25 Raul Fernandez, "Uploading American Politics," *Washington Post*, December 9, 2006, p. A19.

26 Richard Saul Wurman, *Information Anxiety* (New York: Doubleday, 1989), p. 1.

27 See Guy Sorman, *The Empire of Lies* (New York: Encounter Books, 2008).

28 Clay Shirky, "Power Laws, Weblogs and Inequality," February 8, 2003, http://www.shirky.com/writings/powerlaw_weblog.html.

CHAPTER TWO: THE UNFAIRNESS DOCTRINE

1 Quoted in Byron York, "An Unfair Doctrine," *National Review*, July 30, 2007, cover story.

2 Dennis Patrick and Thomas W. Hazlett, "The Return of the Speech Police," *Wall Street Journal*, July 30, 2007, p. A13.

3 Nat Hentoff, "The History and Possible Revival of the Fairness Doctrine," *Imprimis*, January 2006, p. 4.

4 See Thomas W. Hazlett, "The Fairness Doctrine and the First Amendment," *Public Interest*, Summer 1989, pp. 103–16.

5 Fred W. Friendly, *The Good Guys, the Bad Guys, and the First Amendment: Free Speech vs. Fairness in Broadcasting* (New York: Random House, 1976), pp. 39–42.

6 Jessie Walker, "Tuning Out Free Speech," *American Conservative*, April 23, 2007, http://www.amconmag.com/2007/2007_04_23/article3.html.

7 Hazlett, "The Fairness Doctrine and the First Amendment," pp. 105–6.

8 *National Broadcasting Co. v. United States*, 319 U.S. 190 (1943).

9 Hazlett, "The Fairness Doctrine and the First Amendment," p. 107.

10 *Telecommunications Research & Action Center v. Federal Communications Commission*, 801 F.2d 501 (D.C. Cir.), *petition for reh'g en banc denied*, 806 F.2d 1115 (D.C. Cir. 1986), *cert. denied*, 482 U.S. 918 (1987); *Branch v. Federal Communications Commission*, 824 F.2d 37 (D.C. Cir.),

cert. denied, 485 U.S. 959 (1988); *Meredith Corp. v. Federal Communications Commission*, 809 F.2d 863 (D.C. Cir. 1987).

11 Ithiel de Sola Pool, *Technologies of Freedom* (Cambridge, Mass.: Harvard University Press), 1983, p. 141.

12 *Red Lion Broadcasting Co. v. FCC*, 395 U.S. 367 (1969).

13 Monroe quoted in John Fund, "'Fairness' Is Foul," OpinionJournal, *Wall Street Journal*, October 29, 2007, http://www.opinionjournal.com/diary/?id=110010795.

14 Peter Huber, *Law and Disorder in Cyberspace: Abolish the FCC and Let Common Law Rule the Telecosm* (Oxford: Oxford University Press, 1997), p. 147.

15 Dennis Patrick, unedited transcript, National Press Club, Washington, D.C., July 18, 2007, http://www.iep.gmu.edu/documents/Patrick.Speech.07.18.07.pdf.

16 Ronald Reagan, "Message to the Senate Returning without Approval the Fairness in Broadcasting Bill," June 19, 1987, http://www.reagan.utexas.edu/archives/speeches/1987/061987h.html.

17 See Thomas W. Hazlett and David W. Sosa, "Was the Fairness Doctrine a 'Chilling Effect'? Evidence from the Postderegulation Radio Market," *Journal of Legal Studies*, vol. 26, no. 1, 1997, pp. 279–301; and the same authors, "Chilling the Internet? Lessons from FCC Regulation of Radio Broadcasting," *Cato Policy Analysis*, no. 270, March 19, 1997.

18 Interview with Adam Bellow, February 2008.

19 Daniel Henninger, "Hillary Talks about 'It,'" OpinionJournal, *Wall Street Journal*, October 11, 2007, http://www.opinionjournal.com/columnists/dhenninger/?id=110010717.

20 Quoted in York, "An Unfair Doctrine."

21 Louise Slaughter and Bill Moyers, "Whatever Happened to Fairness," transcript of *NOW* segment, PBS, December 17, 2004, http://www.pbs.org/now/politics/slaughter.html.

22 Michelle Malkin's blog posting "Fairness Doctrine Watch: The Dem Campaign Continues," June 27, 2007, rounds up a number of revealing statements: http://michellemalkin.com/2007/06/27/fairness-doctrine-watch-the-dem-campaign-continues. See also: The Prowler, "Her Royal Fairness," *The American Spectator*, May 14, 2007, http://www.spectator.org/dsp_article.asp?art_id=11427.

23 The whole exchange was captured on the indispensable Captain's Quarters blog: see "A Colloquy on the Fairness Doctrine," July 13, 2007, http://www.captainsquartersblog.com/mt/archives/010516.php.

Notes

24 Quoted in "Kennedy's Secret Strategy to Stick It to Radio Hosts," a WND editorial on July 11, 2007, http://www.wnd.com/news/article.asp?ARTICLE_ID=56582.

25 See Tim Siglin, "Analysis: EU Issues Paper Threatens Internet Expression Worldwide," Streamingmedia.com, July 13, 2005, http://www.streamingmedia.com/article.asp?id=9103&c=13.

26 "FCC Commissioner: Return Fairness Doctrine Could Control Web Content," http://www.businessandmedia.org/articles/2008/20080812160747.aspx.

27 Franken quoted by John Fund, "'Fairness' Is Foul," OpinionJournal, *Wall Street Journal*, October 29, 2007, http://www.opinionjournal.com/diary/?id=110010795.

28 See John Halprin et al., "The Structural Imbalance of Political Talk Radio," Center for American Progress and Free Press, June 20, 2007.

29 See http://www.barackobama.com/issues/technology.

30 See "47% Favor Government Mandated Political Balance on Radio, TV," Rasmussen Reports, August 14, 2008, http://rasmussenreports.com/public_content/politics/general_politics/47_favor_government_mandated_political_balance_on_radio_tv.

CHAPTER THREE: NETWORK SOCIALISM

1 George Gilder and Bret Swanson, "Estimating the Exaflood," Discovery Institute, January 29, 2008, http://www.discovery.org/a/4428.

2 "Flashback: Hillary Clinton Says Internet Needs 'Rethink,'" Drudge Report, September 25, 2005, http://www.drudgereportarchives.com/data/2005/09/25/20050925_205400_flash4.htm.

3 Interview with George Gilder.

4 Harry C. Alford Jr., "Net Neutrality Is Seen as Benefit for Minorities," letter to the editor, *Wall Street Journal*, February 20, 2008, http://online.wsj.com/article/SB120347191902578837.html; Jose A. Marquez, "Fair Sharing of the Internet's Capabilities," letter to the editor, *Washington Post*, February 21, 2008, http://www.washingtonpost.com/wp-dyn/content/article/2008/02/20/AR2008022002661.html?nav=hcmodule.

5 Interview with Christopher Yoo.

6 Peter Huber, "The Inegalitarian Web," *Forbes*, February 12, 2007, http://www.forbes.com/opinions/free_forbes/2007/0212/094.html.

Notes

7 J. Gregory Sidak, "The Failure of Good Intentions: The WorldCom Fraud and the Collapse of American Telecommunications after Deregulation," *Yale Journal of Regulation*, vol. 20, 2003, pp. 207–67.

8 Quoted in Jennifer Lee, "U.S. Details Ground Rules for Baby Bells and Rivals," *New York Times*, August 22, 2003, p. C2.

9 Richard A. Posner, *Natural Monopoly and Its Regulation*, 30th ed. (Washington, D.C.: Cato Institute, 1999).

10 Alfred E. Kahn, *The Economics of Regulation: Principles and Institutions* (Cambridge, Mass.: MIT Press, 1971), p. 46.

11 Nancy Keenan and Roberta Combs, "Can You Hear Us Now?" *Washington Post*, October 17, 2007, http://www.washingtonpost.com/wp-dyn/content/article/2007/10/16/AR2007101601536.html.

12 "The Verizon Warning," *New York Times*, October 3, 2007, http://www.nytimes.com/2007/10/03/opinion/03wed1.html?_r=3&oref=slogin&oref=slogin&oref=slogin.

13 Laurence H. Tribe, "Freedom of Speech and Press in the 21st Century: New Technology Meets Old Constitutionalism," Progress & Freedom Foundation, *Progress on Point* 14.19, September 2007, http://www.pff.org/issues-pubs/pops/pop14.19tribetranscript.pdf.

CHAPTER FOUR: NEOPHOBIA

1 As Jason Illian, author of *MySpace, MyKids*, notes: "Every time a new medium is introduced, it garners attention. And when problems arise, we are quick to place blame on the new technology, when in reality, the same problems we have always had are simply revealing themselves in new ways." Jason Illian, *MySpace, MyKids* (Eugene, Ore.: Harvest House Publishers, 2007), pp. 19–20. For other examples, see Tom Standage, "Those Darn Kids and Their Darn New Technology," *Wired*, April 2006, pp. 114–15.

2 "Breeding Evil? Defending Video Games," *The Economist*, August 4, 2005, http://www.economist.com/displaystory.cfm?story_id=4247084.

3 See http://clinton.senate.gov/~clinton/speeches/2005314533.html; and http://www.senate.gov/~clinton/news/statements/details.cfm?id=240603.

4 "Parents Increasingly Using ESRB Ratings to Restrict the Video Games Their Children Play," Entertainment Software Rating Board press release, May 4, 2007, http://www.ersb.org/about/news/downloads/ESRB_AwarenessUsePR_5.4.07.pdf.

5 The ESRB keeps a running list of resources for parents at: http://www.esrb.org/about/resources.jsp.

6 "Microsoft, PTA and Super Bowl Champion Jerry Rice Announce New Tools to Help Parents Manage Kids' Interactive Media Use," Microsoft Corp. press release, November 7, 2007, http://www.microsoft.com/presspass/press/2007/nov07/11-07Family TimerPR.mspx.

7 Amanda Lenhart and Mary Madden, *Teens, Privacy, and Online Social Networks*, Pew Internet & American Life Project, April 18, 2007, http://www.pewinternet.org/PPF/r/211/report_display.asp.

8 See Dmitri Williams and Marko Skorik, "Internet Fantasy Violence: A Test of Aggression in an Online Game," *Communication Monographs*, vol. 72, no. 2, June 2005, pp. 217–33.

9 Harold Schechter, *Savage Pastimes: A Cultural History of Violent Entertainment* (New York: St. Martin's Press, 2005), p. 139. Between 1895 and 1955, Schechter notes, seven of the top fifteen best-selling books published in the United States were Mickey Spillane novels.

10 Ibid., pp. 24–25.

11 *American Amusement Machine Association et al. v. Kendrick et al.*, 244 F.3d 572 (7th Cir. 2001), http://caselaw.lp.findlaw.com/scripts/getcase.pl?court=7th&navby=case&no=003643.

12 Aristotle's *Poetics*, trans. S. H. Butcher, Part VI, http://classics.mit.edu/Aristotle/poetics.1.1.html.

13 Ibid., Part IX.

14 For a broader discussion of the catharsis debate from Plato and Aristotle on down to the modern "media effects" psychologists and social scientists, see Marjorie Heins, *Not in Front of the Children: "Indecency," Censorship, and the Innocence of Youth* (New York: Hill & Wang, 2001), pp. 228–53.

15 Gerard Jones, *Killing Monsters: Why Children Need Fantasy, Super Heroes, and Make-Believe Violence* (New York: Basic Books, 2002), p. 11.

16 Steven Johnson, *Everything Bad Is Good for You: How Today's Popular Culture Is Actually Making Us Smarter* (New York: Riverhead Books, 2005), p. 166.

17 Idem, "Watching TV Makes You Smarter," *New York Times Magazine*, April 24, 2005, p. 59.

18 James Paul Gee, *What Video Games Have to Teach Us about Learning and Literacy* (New York: Palgrave, 2003). Also see David Williamson Shaffer, *How Computer Games Help Children Learn* (New York: Palgrave, 2008).

19   See Emery P. Dalesio, "Video Gaming Technology Branching Out, Getting Serious," *USA Today*, August 11, 2004, p. 1.

20   See Reena Jana, "Harnessing the Power of Video Games," *Business-Week*, August 17, 2006, http://www.businessweek.com/innovate/content/aug2006/id20060817_517827.htm.

21   As *The Economist* editorialized: "Novels were once considered too low-brow for university literature courses, but eventually the disapproving professors retired. Waltz music and dancing were condemned in the 19th century; all that was thought to be 'intoxicating' and 'depraved,' and the music was outlawed in some places. Today it is hard to imagine what the fuss was about. And rock and roll was thought to encourage violence, promiscuity and Satanism; but today even grannies buy Coldplay albums." Quoted in "Breeding Evil?" p. 9.

22   "Video games are most threatening to adults who have seen images of them but never tried to play them." Jones, *Killing Monsters*, p. 173.

23   Adam Thierer, "Thinking Seriously about Cable & Satellite Censorship: An Informal Analysis of S-616, the Rockefeller-Hutchison Bill," Progress & Freedom Foundation, *Progress on Point* 12.6, April 2005, http://www.pff.org/issues-pubs/pops/pop12.6 cablecensorship.pdf.

24   *FCC v. Pacifica Foundation*, 438 U.S. 726, 727–8 (1978).

25   Federal Communications Commission, *Twelfth Annual Report on Competition in the Video Market*, MB Docket no. 05-255, February 10, 2006, p. 4, http://hraunfoss.fcc.gov/edocs_public/attachmatch/FCC-06-11A1.pdf.

26   Adam Thierer, "Kid-Friendly Tiering Mandates: More Government Nannyism for Cable TV," Progress & Freedom Foundation, *Progress Snapshot* 1.2, May 2005, http://www.pff.org/issues-pubs/ps/ps1.2familyfriendlytiering.pdf.

27   "Religious Broadcasters Oppose FCC Chairman's Call for Pay-per-Channel Legislation," press release, Faith and Family Broadcasting Coalition, April 17, 2007, http://www.ncta.com/DocumentBinary.aspx?id=575. The late Rev. Jerry Falwell also opposed à la carte regulation for the same reason, saying: "Though well-intentioned, the fact is that à la carte would threaten the very existence of religious broadcasting and the vital ministry conducted over the television airwaves." Quoted in Ted Hearn, "Falwell's 11th Commandment: No à la Carte," *Multichannel News*, November 17, 2004, http://www.multichannel.com/article/CA481169.html.

28   Declan McCullagh, "Chat Rooms Could Face Expulsion," CNet

News.com, July 28, 2006, http://news.cnet.com/
2100-1028_3-6099414.html.

29 See Emily Steel and Julia Angwin, "MySpace Receives More Pressure
to Limit Children's Access to Site," *Wall Street Journal*, June 23, 2006,
http://online.wsj.com/public/article/
SB115102268445288250-YRxktorTsyyfiQiQf2
EPBYSf7iU_20070624.html?mod=tff_main_tff_top.

30 Kellie Wilson, "Kentucky Lawmaker Wants to Make Anonymous
Internet Posting Illegal," WTVQ.com, May 5, 2008,
http://www.wtvq.com/content/midatlantic/tvq/
video.apx.-content-articles-TVQ-2008-03-05-0011.html.

31 Andrea J. Sedlak, David Finkelhor, Heather Hammer, and Dana J.
Schultz, "National Estimate of Missing Children: An Overview,"
*National Incidence Studies of Missing, Abducted, Runaway, and
Thrownaway Children* (NISMART), October 2002, p. 7,
http://www.missingkids.com/cn_US/documents/nismart2_
overview.pdf.

32 A recent study of cases about missing children in Ohio revealed a similar trend. Of the 11,074 documented missing-child cases in 2005, just
five involved abduction by strangers compared with 146 abductions by
family members. 2005 Annual Report, Ohio Missing Children Clear-
inghouse, p. 4, http://www.ag.state.oh.us/victim/pubs/
2005ann_rept_mcc.pdf.

33 Janis Wolak, David Finkelhor, and Kimberly Mitchell, "Internet-
Initiated Sex Crimes against Minors: Implications for Prevention
Based on Findings from a National Study," *Journal of Adolescent Health*,
vol. 35, no. 5, 2004, pp. 11–20, http://www.unh.edu/ccrc/pdf/
CV71.pdf.

34 Nancy E. Willard, *Cyber-Safe Kids, Cyber-Savvy Teens* (San Francisco:
Jossey-Bass, 2007), pp. 155–56.

35 Janis Wolak, Kimberly Mitchell, and David Finkelhor, *Online Victim-
ization: Five Years Later*, National Center for Missing and Exploited
Children, 2006, http://www.missingkids.com/en_US/
publications/NC167.pdf.

36 Steel and Angwin, "MySpace Receives More Pressure to Limit Children's Access to Site."

37 See Adam Thierer, "Social Networking and Age Verification: Many
Hard Questions; No Easy Solutions," Progress & Freedom Foundation,
Progress on Point 14.5, March 2007, http://www.pff.org/issues-pubs/
pops/pop14.5ageverification.pdf.

38 Idem, "Child Protection and the Internet: The '3-E' Solution (Empower, Educate & Enforce)," submitted to the Advisory Committee of the Congressional Internet Caucus, 2006, http://www.netcaucus.org/books/childsafety2006/pff.pdf.

39 Quoted in Anick Jesdanun, "Age Verification at Social-Network Sites Could Prove Difficult," *Associated Press Financial Wire*, July 14, 2006.

40 Nancy Willard echoes the point: "With the expanded ability to meet and interact with new people online comes the need for a new skill— online stranger literacy. Online stranger literacy is the ability to determine the trustworthiness and safety of individuals who are unknown in person, with whom one is communicating online. It is the 'people' equivalent of information literacy." *Cyber-Safe Kids, Cyber-Savvy Teens*, p. 120.

41 Quoted in Jesdanun, "Age Verification at Social Network Sites Could Prove Difficult."

42 Parry Aftab, filing in COPPA Rule Review 2005 before the Federal Trade Commission, June 27, 2005, p. 4.

43 See Jessica E. Vascellaro and Anjali Athavaley, "Foley Scandal Turns Parents into Web Sleuths," *Wall Street Journal*, October 18, 2006, p. D1.

44 Anne Barnard, "MySpace Agrees to Lead Fight to Stop Sex Predators," *New York Times*, January 15, 2008, http://www.nytimes.com/2008/01/15/us/15myspace.html?ref=us; Adam Thierer, "The MySpace-AG Agreement: A Model Code of Conduct for Social Networking?" Progress & Freedom Foundation, *Progress on Point* 15.1, January 2008, http://www.pff.org/issues-pubs/pops/pop15.1myspaceAGagreement.pdf.

45 "5 Percent of Sex Offenders Rearrested for Another Sex Crime within 3 Years of Prison Release," U.S. Department of Justice, Office of Justice Programs, November 16, 2003, http://www.ojp.usdoj.gov/bjs/pub/press/rsorp94pr.htm.

46 "President Signs H.R. 4472, the Adam Walsh Child Protection and Safety Act of 2006," White House press release, July 27, 2006, http://www.whitehouse.gov/news/releases/2006/07/20060727-6.html.

47 Adam Thierer, "Convergence-Era Content Regulation? S. 602, 'The Child Safe Viewing Act of 2007,'" Progress & Freedom Foundation, *Progress on Point* 14.17, August 2007, http://www.pff.org/issues-pubs/pops/pop14.17pryorchildsafetyviewingact.pdf.

Notes

CHAPTER FIVE: CAMPAIGN-FINANCE REFORM'S WAR
ON POLITICAL SPEECH

1 George Will, "Free Speech under Siege," *Newsweek*, December 5, 2005, http://www.newsweek.com/id/51375. Will has been an eloquent —and persistent—critic of campaign-finance regulations.

2 Jonathan Rauch, "Here's a New Campaign Finance Reform Plan: Just Stop," *National Journal*, May 7, 2005.

3 This and later statements by Justice Thomas are quoted from his remarkable dissent in *McConnell v. Federal Election Commission* (2003).

4 See Bradley A. Smith, "Campaign Finance Reform's War on Political Freedom," *City Journal*, July 1, 2007, http://www.city-journal.org/html/ws2007-07-01bs.html. For more on the history, see Smith's masterful *Unfree Speech: The Folly of Campaign Finance Reform* (Princeton, N.J.: Princeton University Press, 2001).

5 Ryan Sager, "Buying 'Reform,'" *New York Post*, March 17, 2005, p. 33.

6 Quoted in Smith, "Campaign Finance Reform's War on Political Freedom."

7 See John Samples, *The Fallacy of Campaign Finance Reform* (Chicago: University of Chicago Press, 2006), especially Part One, which contrasts the Madisonian conception of politics with the progressive tradition.

8 See Edward Foley, "Equal-Dollars-per-Voter: A Constitutional Principle of Campaign Finance," *Columbia Law Review*, vol. 94, no. 4, 1994; Richard L. Hasen, "Campaign Finance Laws and the Rupert Murdoch Problem," *Texas Law Review*, June 1999, http://papers.ssrn.com/sol3/papers.cfm?abstract_id=139581; Ronald Dworkin, "The Curse of American Politics," *New York Review of Books*, October 17, 1996, p. 19.

9 Quoted in "McCain-Feingold, RIP," *Wall Street Journal*, December 4, 2002, p. A18.

10 John Samples and Adam D. Thierer, "Why Subsidize the Soapbox?: The McCain Free Airtime Proposal and the Future of Broadcasting," Cato Institute, *Policy Analysis* no. 480, August 6, 2003, http://www.cato.org/pubs/pas/pa480.pdf.

11 This and later comments by Michael Toner are from: http://electionlawblog.org/archives/toner2.doc.

12 The comments can be accessed at: http://www.campaignlegalcenter.org/attachments/1428.pdf.

13 See Bob Bauer's post, "Thanksgiving in Cyberpolitics," on his More

Notes

Soft Money Hard Law website:
http://www.moresoftmoneyhardlaw.com/updates/other_related_legal_
developments.html?Archive=1&AID=550.

14 Bradley A. Smith, "Campaign Finance Reform: Searching for Corruption in All the Wrong Places," *Cato Supreme Court Review
2002–2003* (Washington, D.C.: Cato Institute, 2003), pp. 187–223.

15 Idem, "Campaign Finance Reform's War on Political Freedom."

16 Adam Thierer, "The 'Rathergate' Incident: Remembering Why Sepa-
ration of Press and State Is Vital," Cato Institute, *Tech Knowledge*
no. 88, September 30, 2004, http://www.cato.org/tech/tk/
040930-tk-2.html.

17 Interview with Kirby Wilbur.

18 Interview with Bill Maurer.

19 Smith, "Campaign Finance Reform's War on Political Freedom."

20 Reynolds made the comment at a Politics Online Conference in
March 2005; for a transcript, see http://www.redstate.com/story/
2005/3/20/84959/3905.

21 Thomas Sowell, "The Facts vs. 'Campaign Finance Reform' Fictions,"
Capitalism Magazine, April 13, 2001, http://www.capmag.com/
article.asp?ID=472.

22 McCain quoted by John Samples, "McCain vs. Madison," *The
American Spectator*, January 15, 2008,
http://www.spectator.org/dsp_article.asp?art_id=12575.

23 Smith, "Campaign Finance Reform: Searching for Corruption in All
the Wrong Places," p. 200.

24 See Ed Morrisey's posting "Mr. Clean?" on the Captain's Quarters
blog, http://www.captainsquartersblog.com/mt/archives/004010.php.

25 Smith, "Campaign Finance Reform's War on Political Freedom." See
also John Samples, "'Enough Is Enough,'" National Review Online,
June 26, 2007, http://article.nationalreview.com/?q=MzM2ODI5
YWM2Y2MiMDIwZjEzNWU3MDMyM2Y3YmRkODg=.

26 Bradley A. Smith and Steve Simpson, "Unfettered Speech, Now,"
Washington Post, February 16, 2008, p. A21.

CONCLUSION

1 Peter Huber, *Orwell's Revenge: The 1984 Palimpsest* (New York: Free
Press, 1994), p. 239.

2 Ibid., p. 197.

INDEX

Index

Index

Index

Index

Index

Index

A NOTE ON THE TYPE

A MANIFESTO FOR MEDIA FREEDOM *has been set in Caslon,
a type that ranks among the most enduring and influential faces in
the history of English typefounding. Derived from Dutch types of
the late seventeenth century, the types cut by William Caslon and
issued in his famed 1734 specimen formed the basis of the Caslon
family's fortunes as typefounders. The Caslon types occupy an
important place in the history of type design, standing as they do at
the end of the development of old-style types and looking forward to
the rise of transitional and modern types. The types enjoyed an extraordinary popularity that lasted well into the nineteenth century—
many foundries produced pirated versions over the years—and
while they were eventually eclipsed by modern faces by mid-century,
they would ultimately play an important role in the revival of fine
printing in the late 1800s. In its original form and in its many later
iterations, the esteem Caslon earned among printers and readers on
both sides of the Atlantic is undeniable: it was chosen for the first
appearance in type of the Declaration of Independence, and George
Bernard Shaw insisted that all his books be printed in Caslon.*

DESIGN & COMPOSITION BY CARL W. SCARBROUGH